Queerness
IN THE
Catholic Church

Queerness IN THE Catholic Church

Wanted, Loved, Blessed

Edited by Wolfgang F. Rothe
Translated by Patrick Conlin

Paulist Press
New York / Mahwah, NJ

Scripture quotations are from New Revised Standard Version Bible: Catholic Edition, copyright © 1989, 1993 National Council of the Churches of Christ in the United States of America. Used by permission. All rights reserved worldwide.

Cover image: composite image/artwork designed by Sharyn Banks
Cover design by Sharyn Banks
Book design by Lynn Else

English language copyright © 2024 by Paulist Press

Initially published in Germany as *Gewollt. Geliebt. Gesegnet. Queer-Sein in der katholischen Kirche* edited by Wolfgang F. Rothe © 2022 Verlag Herder GmbH, Freiburg im Breisgau.

All rights reserved. No part of this publication may be reproduced, stored in a retrieval system, or transmitted in any form or by any means, electronic, mechanical, photocopying, recording, scanning, or otherwise, without either the prior written permission of the Publisher, or authorization through payment of the appropriate per-copy fee to the Copyright Clearance Center, Inc., www.copyright.com. Requests to the Publisher for permission should be addressed to the Permissions Department, Paulist Press, permissions@paulistpress.com.

Library of Congress Cataloging-in-Publication Data
Names: Rothe, Wolfgang F., author. | Conlin, Patrick, translator.
Title: Queerness in the Catholic church : wanted, loved, blessed / edited by Wolfgang F. Rothe ; translated by Patrick Conlin.
Other titles: Gewollt, Geliebt, Gesegnet. English
Description: New York ; Mahwah, NJ : Paulist Press, [2024] | "Originally published in Germany as Gewollt. Geliebt. Gesegnet. Queer-Sein in der katholischen Kirche edited by Wolfgang F. Rothe, 2022 Verlag Herder GmbH, Freiburg im Breisgau." | Summary: "The conversation in Germany about LGBTQIA+ Catholics is already happening; this book allows Americans to listen to them as well as to encourage similar conversations in America"—Provided by publisher.
Identifiers: LCCN 2023020536 (print) | LCCN 2023020537 (ebook) | ISBN 9780809156658 (paperback) | ISBN 9780809188260 (ebook)
Subjects: LCSH: Catholic sexual minorities. | Homosexuality—Religious aspects—Catholic Church. | Church work with sexual minorities.
Classification: LCC BX1795.H66 G4913 2024 (print) | LCC BX1795.H66 (ebook) | DDC 261.8/35766—dc23/eng/20230928
LC record available at https://lccn.loc.gov/2023020536
LC ebook record available at https://lccn.loc.gov/2023020537

ISBN 978-0-8091-5665-8 (paperback)
ISBN 978-0-8091-8826-0 (e-book)

Published by Paulist Press
997 Macarthur Boulevard
Mahwah, New Jersey 07430
www.paulistpress.com

Printed and bound in the
United States of America

Contents

Foreword by Bishop John Stowe, OFM Conv. xi

Acknowledgments xv

Introduction xvii

My Faith, My Gayness, My Fears 1
    Anonymous

My Best Friend Disowned Me Because of
    My Homosexuality 3
    Nico Abrell

I Hid Behind the Façade of Conservative Catholicism 5
    Anonymous

Memories—Speechlessness—Dreams/Spaces of Faith 8
    Marian Antoni

God Created Me the Way I Am 11
    Charlotte Baron

I Am Gay and Catholic—So What? 13
    Jan Baumann

How I Met God as a Gay Scientist 16
    Dr. Arturo Blázquez Navarro

Contents

How the Church Makes Life Difficult for My Wife 18
Anonymous

Finding the Strength to Come Out 20
Anonymous

Catholic Means Universal and That Includes Everyone 22
Verena Eitzenberger

The Beam in the Eye 25
Dr. Johannes zu Eltz

Closest Loves Like Yourself 27
Johannes Engelhardt

Examination of Conscience 29
Lukas Färber

Why Are We Still Catholic as a Rainbow Family? 31
Ulrike Fasching

The "Gay Lobby" in the Vatican—Fact or Fiction? 33
Ingo-Michael Feth

Confiteor—Convertere 36
Joachim Frank

How a Selfie with "Prince Charming" Changed My Life..... 39
Henry Frömmichen

World Church on Site 41
Dieter Geerlings

A Gay Couple in the Church for Five Decades 44
Manfred Hassemer-Tiedeken

God Has a Plan for Me as a Gay Man 47
Dr. Andreas Helfrich

When Two Men Love Each Other, That's Just Love 49
Markus Helfrich

Contents

A Gay Man Opened My Door to the Church 52
    Simone Hock

For a Long Time, I Felt My Homosexuality
Was a Sin and Shame 55
    Giovanni Inzerilli

Good News for My People 57
    Matthias Katsch

Standing Up for LGBTQIA+ People in the Church 60
    Dr. Julia Knop

Love Is the Visible Blessing of God in the World 63
    Lisa Kötter

I Want to Become A Priest, But… 66
    Anonymous

I Believed That I Wasn't Allowed to Be Gay 69
    Christoph Krenzel

Two Gay Boys in Our Family 72
    Ulrike Krenzel

Homosexuality as a Weapon 75
    Ulrich Küchl

We All Need Tolerance 78
    Anonymous

The Church's Sexual Morality and Its Victims 81
    Michael Kurz

Before God, I Can Be Who I Am 84
    Anonymous

I Am Grateful to the Church—And Struggle
with It 86
    Michael Langer

Contents

I Want You to Be Happy 89
    Patrick Lindner

The Brother's* Distress 92
    Gudrun Lux

The Rainbow Is a Bridge between Heaven and Earth 95
    Fady Maalouf

God Is Love 98
    Christof Gabriel Maetze

Agape and *Eros*—Two Sides of the Same Coin 100
    Anonymous

My Child Is Transgender—What's Wrong with That? 102
    Iris Molsbeck

Praying It Away Doesn't Work 105
    Anonymous

Why I Am Not Catholic, Unlike My Wife 108
    Almut Münster

Better to Resign from the Priesthood than to
Lead a Double Life 110
    Otto Johann Piplics

Why I Do Not Need Any Church 113
    Ansgar Pippel

I Am a Learner 115
    Gregor Podschun

"But If I Do Not Have Love…" 118
    Peter Priller

Three Days in Spring 121
    Dr. Matthias Remenyi

Contents

My Lesbian Daughter Can Be Sure of My Love
   and of God's Love 124
    Katrin Richthofer

God Called Me to Be Gay and a Priest 127
    Anonymous

I Lived behind a Mask for a Long Time 130
    Anonymous

The Church Rejects Me as Trans—My Parish Doesn't 132
    Cleo Schmitz

When No One Can Hear You Scream 135
    Dr. Ruben Schneider

Quo Vadis? 138
    Anonymous

My Gay "Little" Brother 140
    Dr. Thomas Schüller

Doubt, Love, and the Incomplete Basilica of St. Peter 143
    Martin Speer

Don't Be Afraid of Change 145
    Andreas Sturm

Homophobia in God's Name Is Spiritual Abuse 148
    Anonymous

Telling My Lesbian Daughter That Being a Catholic
   Is Liberating 151
    Christian Taufenbach

Hoping for a Miracle 154
    Stefan Theierl

Faith Is a Part of Who I Am—Just Like Being Gay 156
    Stefan Thurner

Contents

Encounter Creates Change 159
    Heinrich Timmerevers

God's Love Calls Me to Love My Wife 162
    Anonymous

Committed to the Christian Image of Humanity 164
    Alexander Vogt

Sanctuary and Snare 167
    Anonymous

Queer Life Trusting in God 170
    Dr. Christine Waltner

My Faith Gives Me the Strength to Live with HIV 172
    Manfred Weber

I Feel Abandoned by the Church 174
    Anonymous

The Lord God Wants Me as I Am 176
    Anonymous

Foreword

The *Vademecum* (Handbook) produced by the Vatican Office of the Synod for the multiphase Synod on Synodality proclaimed by Pope Francis, insists that the first moment of the Synod be focused on listening. The very concept of synodality had largely been lost in the western Church although Pope Paul VI formally reestablished the Synod of Bishops following the Second Vatican Council. It is not surprising that the very word *synod* is still relatively unknown by many Catholics, and even among those who are engaged in the synod process, clarity about how synodality works and how it might transform the Church is often lacking. For good reason, the synod begins with listening.

> The objective of the current Synod is to listen, as the entire People of God, to what the Holy Spirit is saying to the Church. We do so by listening together to the Word of God in Scripture and the living Tradition of the Church, and then by listening to one another, and especially to those at the margins, discerning the signs of the times. In fact, the whole Synodal Process aims at fostering a lived experience of discernment, participation, and co-responsibility, where a diversity of gifts is brought together for the Church's mission in the world. [*For a Synodal Church: Communion, Participation and Mission. Vademecum for the*

Queerness IN THE Catholic Church

Synod on Synodality. The Vatican: Secretary General of the Synod, 2021. Sec 1.3]

Fr. Wolfgang Rothe has done this kind of listening extensively and is inviting us to do so as well through the printed page. He has gone to an important portion of the Church's membership on the margins by engaging in conversation with people who identify as queer and who also have some relationship with the Catholic Church, mostly as members. Listening, by reading these accounts of personal experience by Catholics whose identity has been condemned, ignored, shamed, ridiculed, excluded, and even deemed nonexistent, is an eye-opening exercise that is essential to the synodal process and for being faithful to the example of Jesus in the life of the Church today.

The subtitle of this collection of painfully honest essays expresses an aspiration for how the Church should look upon our queer members: wanted, loved, blessed. What a wonderful and very faithful starting point for our way of relating to every member of the Body of Christ, and especially to those whose story reveals that they have not often felt wanted, not only unloved but rejected because of who they love, and so unblessed that they are part of the only class of people that the Dicastery of the Doctrine of the Faith says cannot be officially blessed. The vision contained in that subtitle is really an application of a fundamental truth of our faith, that each of us is made in the image and likeness of God.

The reader here is invited into the sacred space of the lived experience of other members of the Body of Christ. Some of these members are active in ministry, in pursuing a deeper understanding of the faith, in advocating for a more just society even within the Church. Others are quietly pursuing their relationship with God, not feeling free enough to be themselves in the Church community. Others have quite literally been driven away from the Church by those whose own zeal-

Foreword

otry for the faith have blinded them to the merciful and compassionate God of love revealed by Jesus Christ.

The stories contained here reveal pain and rejection far too often for a community that describes itself as catholic. They reveal a heroic perseverance in the journey of faith and the community of faith. They also reveal the pain of loved ones who do not self-identify as queer, but cannot get over the contradiction between the message of Jesus and what their loved ones experience in the Church he founded. Occasionally these stories reveal a sense of fullness of belonging and dignity against all odds.

Fr. Rothe's book comes at a critical time. Despite significant backlashes and outbreaks of homophobia, society at large is coming to accept the reality of queerness and to understand that it is not a threat. Some churches are experiencing denominational splits over the place of homosexual and transgender members and clergy. Catholic teaching has been static with its insistence that LGBTQIA+ persons have full dignity and there is no justification for discrimination, but that homosexual activity is intrinsically evil because it cannot possibly lead to procreation. So much of society and our sense of normal is evolving after experiencing a global pandemic, and many people are reevaluating their relationship to institutions and communities among so many other aspects of their life. It is certainly a time for building and rebuilding relationships and for learning to listen attentively to those that we encounter.

The best part of our Catholic tradition has always paid attention to human experience and the multiplicity of ways that God reveals God's self, often to our surprise. This collection contributes to this tradition at a time when we are once again learning to listen so that we can walk together.

Bishop John Stowe, OFM Conv.
June 8, 2023

Acknowledgments

First and foremost, I would like to thank the individual contributors to this book. I would like to thank them for their openness, their willingness to collaborate, and, above all, their contributions, which are as impressive as they are touching. I thank them for the courage they have shown, for the straightforward cooperation, and for the many trusting discussions.

I thank Sr. Philippa Rath, OSB, who set the standard with her book *Because God So Wills It*, in which she let those who had experienced doctrinal discrimination speak for themselves and thereby moved so many. I thank her for encouraging me and for giving me her "blessing" on my book project that could not have come about without her inspiration.

I would also like to thank Herder Publishing and, in particular, chief editor Simon Biallowons for his interested and critical support of this project and his encouraging early interest in publishing it. I especially thank the supervising editor, who accompanied me along the path from manuscript to finished book with a great deal of patience and expertise.

Traudi Heigl thankfully took on the trouble of proofreading. I would like to thank her and many others from my circle of friends—especially Christina "Witch" Fürbass—for all their useful suggestions, countless encouraging words, and so much good advice. And, finally, I thank the one to whom everything is already owed: *Deo gratias*!

Introduction

Lesbian, gay, bisexual, transgender, and other queer people in the Catholic Church! There aren't any! There can't be any! There mustn't be any! And if there are any—for God's sake—then they should kindly keep that to themselves. At least that's what the Vatican wants.

But they are there: lesbian, gay, bisexual, transgender, and other queer people in the Catholic Church. They are there—for God's sake. They are there because God wants them to be, because God so wants them and so created them. But exactly as the Vatican wants, they are often invisible in the Church for who they are and as they are.

They are there; they take part in Mass; they hold offices within the Church and carry out liturgical duties; they play the organ and sing in the church choir; they engage in church groups and committees; they help at parish festivals, youth camps, and seniors' afternoons; and they dutifully pay their Church tax. But they are only partly there; they are allowed to be only partly there.

For a part of them has to be left out, has to be kept secret, denied, and repressed. For this part of them has no place in the Church. This part is their gender identity and/or their sexual orientation and is, therefore, something that is generally of prime importance to what makes them a person, and their identity and orientation are essential to their personality and everything else in their lives.

Queerness IN THE Catholic Church

Meanwhile many of them are no longer here, having been turned away by the Catholic Church, having explained their leaving the Church, having lost their faith, or having moved to another denomination, which doesn't question either who they are or how they are and one where they can be who they really are and welcomed as they are.

Others have withdrawn into niches and safe spaces in the Church that have been opened to them, graciously created for them, or that they have made for themselves. Such safe spaces have certainly served their purpose and are justified, but they contain the risk of ghettoization, isolation, and renewed invisibility.

Still others, for better or worse, have resigned to staying invisible in the Church, remaining who they really are and just as they are. They either feel required or have determined to keep their gender identity and/or sexual orientation to themselves and only bring it up, if at all, outside the Church.

Regardless of whether they leave the Church forever, have come to terms with the small loopholes the Church grants them, or have determined to remain hidden within the Church, their relationship to the Church is always shaped by fractions, rejections, or tensions and therefore leaves them with injuries, hurts, and sorrow.

This suffering is real—as opposed to what causes this suffering. This suffering is caused, namely, by a sexual morality based on assumptions and assertions that often have little to do with reality. The allegedly sacrosanct norms of natural law that the Church claims it must submit to are, above all, simply unnatural.

This is because they are not based on the unbiased perception of nature and natural conditions but on conditions and criteria that are subordinate to both. As a result, nature is perceived through the supposed natural law as if through

Introduction

glasses that narrow the perspective, forcing it into an unnatural corset.

It starts with gender identity. According to the *Catechism of the Catholic Church*, every human being is either male or female—and only male or only female, clearly and unalterably. "Everyone, man and woman, should acknowledge and accept his sexual *identity*" (CCC 2333).

There is no place in this schema for people who define themselves neither as (only) male nor as (only) female. The same is true for people who cannot identify with the gender assigned to them at birth, regardless of the circumstances, assumptions, and decisions on which this assignment may have been based.

This is nothing but a denial of reality. For there are such people. They are real. And just as real is their gender identity, which is for only them to define. And so, these people—just the way they are, just the way they define themselves, and just the way they live according to their nature—are wanted, created, and loved by God.

The same applies to people whose sexual orientation does not correspond to what has been declared the sole norm by the magisterium of the Catholic Church. It is once again far from reality when the "psychological genesis" of homosexuality in the *Catechism of the Catholic Church*—in contrast to heterosexuality—is presented as in need of explanation (cf. CCC 2357).

No less far from reality is the assertion made in the scriptures where homosexuality is "condemned as a serious depravity." The relevant Bible passages do speak of same-sex relations, especially prostitution and sexual assault, but not of homosexual orientation, homosexual love, and homosexual partnership.

It is all the further from reality when the *Catechism of the Catholic Church* thoughtlessly asserts that "most" homosexual people consider their sexual orientation a "trial." If homosexual people—not least of all, homosexual Catholics—see something as a trial, then it is at best discrimination toward them.

And that's why it seems to be the maximum level of detachment from reality when the *Catechism of the Catholic Church* demands that homosexual people are generally "called to chastity"—chastity in the sense of complete sexual abstinence. Once again, this denies and degrades the nature of the individuals involved.

Considering such a concentrated detachment from reality, it is time to make queer people visible in the Church and for the Church to give them a voice, to let them speak. Exactly this—no more and no less—is the concern of this book. It offers insights into the lived reality of Catholic or formerly Catholic people with an LGBTQIA+ background.

As noted earlier, the direct model for this was the book *Because God So Wills It*, published in early 2021, where the Benedictine nun Philippa Roth has collected contributions from women who feel called to be Catholic priests but who, considering the magisterium's "no" to the ordination of women, cannot live out their vocation, or can only to a limited extent, or, perhaps better, can only outside the ecclesiastical order.

Even people who—like myself—no longer needed to be convinced that the reasons given by the magisterium against the ordination of women are worse than threadbare were stirred and shaken up in a lasting manner by this book. One can isolate oneself from knowledge; experiences, however, seep through.

Beyond all the reasons that could be given for and against the ordination of women, this book has made it clear that ultimately it is not nor should it be about an abstract question, nor about traditions, teachings, and decrees, but about concrete people and their destiny, about their unrecognized vocations, destroyed hopes, and blocked paths of life.

Introduction

It's no different for queer people in the Catholic Church: they too are forbidden by the Church to live out their vocation—their vocation to a completely normal queer life in the Catholic Church. They too must accept that they cannot live out their vocation or must hide or withdraw into some niche.

That must change. Things can change, however, only if we no longer simply talk *about* those concerned but finally also talk *with* them. It can change only if those concerned share, if they bring up their disappointments, injuries, and sufferings, but also their longings, hopes, and demands.

That is exactly what happens in this book: queer people who are or were Catholic share their feelings, experiences, and journeys. For some, this was a need: it seemed like they were only waiting finally to be able to tell their stories; others, however, were noticeably difficult—they tarried, didn't respond at all, or declined.

Both reactions are understandable. It is noteworthy, however, that most of the people who were invited agreed and ultimately took part, whereas only a few did not respond or declined. This alone shows that the time is ripe for this. The lived reality of queer people in the Catholic Church is not a marginal issue; it is about the Church's right to exist.

The weal and woe of minorities, especially of discriminated and marginalized minorities, is ultimately the measuring stick of Christianity and thus also the measuring stick of Catholicism. Christ did not write a catechism or code of canon law but provided "an example that you should do as I have done for you" (John 13:15)—indeed, an example of appreciation, respect, and love.

When I began working on this book, I became aware for the first time how many queer people I know, how many queer people live and work in my neighborhood, how many queer people there are in general—and indeed even queer Catholics.

Queerness IN THE Catholic Church

It was they who first asked me if they would be able to participate.

In a second step, I asked the queer Catholics I already knew if they had any acquaintances who would come and be interviewed for my work. And in a third step, I finally turned to various organizations, groups, and communities of queer Catholics and so expanded the radius still further.

Over time, however, a considerable number of people contacted me who, in one way or another, had heard or read about this book project and were now asking if they could participate in it. Several of them even sent along a complete article. I also warmly welcomed them and their articles.

The picture that emerged is as colorful as it is complex. There is not "one" feeling, experience, or journey of queer Catholics. There are queer Catholics who have come to terms with their Church, there are queer Catholics who struggle and are at odds with their Church, and there are queer Catholics who have distanced themselves from the Church or broken from it.

And there are not only Catholics or former Catholics who are directly affected. Every Catholic directly affected is surrounded by people who are indirectly affected, if in varying degrees: parents, grandparents, siblings, children, partners, friends, colleagues, pastors, and many others.

They too must deal with and come to terms with the identity and life of the affected, as well as the related traditions, teachings, and commandments of the Catholic Church. And this is often difficult for them. But not for this reason alone are they also part of the reality that needs to be perceived and accepted. And therefore, they also have their say in this book.

Due to the degradation, discrimination, and marginalization that queer people experience in the Catholic Church, it was important to give everyone who wanted to participate in this project the opportunity to remain anonymous from

Introduction

the outset. The reasons for that may be diverse, but they are always valid.

Their remaining anonymous takes nothing from the articles' meaningfulness and value. On the contrary, the desire or, rather, the need (e.g., for professional reasons) to remain anonymous is part of reality. This makes clear once again the pressure these people are under and the fears to which they are exposed.

My efforts to ensure at least a reasonably balanced relationship between nonbinary, female, and male authors have largely remained unsuccessful. It also seems to be part of reality that female and nonbinary people in the Catholic Church find it even more difficult than males to openly admit their identity.

The same seems to be true for queer people of advanced age. It is probably due to the social developments of the last few decades that young people find it much easier to talk about being queer. If so, there is reason for hope, because the Church will not be able to shield itself completely from these developments.

As far as the structure of the book is concerned, no distinction was made between the different perspectives from which the individual articles were written. In the same way, numbering them was intentionally foregone. The articles were simply arranged in alphabetical order according to the last names of the authors.

What began as purely a book project over time also became a pastoral project. Many of the authors felt the need to tell me their stories personally—be it on the phone or face-to-face. They could not be stopped by the fact that some had to travel for this purpose.

Many tears were shed during these talks—tears of sorrow, but also tears of redemption. The same might have happened while some of the articles were being written. I hope that this may also be the case when reading the articles: that the readers will feel the suffering of those affected and will accordingly work to redeem them of their suffering, their fear, and their pressure.

A sexual morality that creates pressure, fear, and suffering instead of protecting against such things is no morality. It may call itself morality, but it is deeply immoral. Above all, however, it is not Christian and, to that extent, is also not Catholic. For it to become Christian and Catholic again, it needs a fundamental change of perspective. That is what I hope to contribute with this book.

My Faith, My Gayness, My Fears

Anonymous
(born in 1990, educator)

My parents named me after an archangel. The Catholic faith is very present in my family. I grew up in a village with almost 350 souls in the Black Forest. Almost everyone there is a Catholic Christian. From an early age, I have regularly attended church services with my mother. After my first communion, I volunteered for many years in my home parish.

By the age of fifteen, I realized that I was "different," that I was emotionally and sexually attracted to boys of my own age. A difficult time began for me when I realized that I was gay: Was being gay compatible with being a faithful Christian? Homosexuality has always been portrayed as abnormal, sick, sinful, evil, and the road to hell in my home parish. But most of the time it wasn't talked about.

I was afraid to come out to my family. And so, at first, I kept my gayness a secret. When my parents weren't around, I would secretly sit down at the computer to see if being gay and being Catholic could somehow be reconciled. The answers I found on the internet didn't reassure me but rather fueled my anxiety. Of course, I found all these passages in the Bible where homosexuality is supposedly regarded as negative and accompanied with radical comments.

As a result, I developed such an overwhelming fear that I first fell into deep sadness, later developed feelings of depression, and finally, shortly before coming of age, was very close to suicide. This had an impact on my entire life at that time. I often skipped school to party with friends. I just wanted to forget.

When I was twenty, I decided to come clean with myself and my faith. I did a year-long vocational training program and started to meditate. It made me suddenly realize that no human being has the right to judge another. This fact is much more important than anything else. At the age of twenty-one, I found the courage to come out to my family and friends. And was lucky enough to be welcomed with open arms.

Therefore, I choose to dedicate my life to humanity. I first trained as a nanny and then as an educator. Today, I am a licensed educator and enjoy working with the children in the kindergarten. The message of love for people motivates me every day.

There is, however, one major concern that I carry. I read that, as an employee of the Catholic Church, you can no longer be fired for homosexuality. It's different, however, if I married. Then there could still be problems.

But the most important thing is that today I know that I am the way that God wanted me to be. And this also applies if one day I should find the man of my life. Because what could be wrong about giving love, loyalty, and care to another person, regardless of gender, for the rest of your life? And when I lie in bed at night and have doubts, I picture Jesus sitting on the edge of my bed, looking at me with a gentle smile and telling me just by his eyes, "I love you—just as you are!"

My Best Friend Disowned Me Because of My Homosexuality

Nico Abrell
(born in 1999, content creator on YouTube, author, and singer-songwriter)

I grew up in a small village in southern Bavaria and always knew that I was different from the other locals. I couldn't really explain why that was, but I never really felt like I belonged.

I grew up believing that a husband belongs to a wife and vice versa, that one must go to church regularly and become an altar boy. And I believed that! I believed what I was told and lived by it. So I became an altar boy and convinced myself that I really liked Anna from the other class. But if I had listened to my heart for a moment, I would have known that I didn't think Anna was as great as Tobias.

Everything was just like a normal (straight) village life — until I met my first boyfriend on YouTube. It was then that I realized for the first time that I definitely would not live up to what was expected of me in my village.

My best friend was also an altar boy and deeply religious. When I told him that I was gay and had fallen in love with a

Queerness IN THE Catholic Church

boy, he broke off the friendship immediately. His reason for this was that he wasn't brought up that way. Our friendship was very closely linked to faith and so my connection to the Church broke with it. I am of the opinion, however, that faith and Church are two different things anyway.

The "good news" about my sexual orientation spread like wildfire in the village at the time, whereupon people showed their contempt, not with words but with looks, and when I approached, they disappeared around the next corner.

Even my mom didn't react very happily at first to my outing. But she also felt like she was the only one in the entire village who understood that I hadn't changed at all. I had legitimately revealed a previously hidden part of myself and presented it to the outside world. I still knew, however, that I was no longer welcome in my home village. I counted the days until my graduation and then moved to Berlin.

The parish itself was not the main reason why I left village life behind, because I can say that I rose above the scornful looks. Nevertheless, I knew that I could not have been truly happy there with my plans and visions for the future.

Nowadays, my relationship to faith is rather splintered. Since my best friend embodied the faith for me, breaking with him also led to a break with the faith. That doesn't mean I don't believe in God and life after death. I do believe that there is some form of afterlife. But I do not believe in a Church that casts people out because of their sexuality. I'm aware that not every denomination, let alone every parish, is homophobic, but the trauma from my childhood still lingers.

I Hid behind the Façade of Conservative Catholicism

Anonymous
(born in 1990, commercial clerk)

It is Sunday morning. I am sitting in the back seat of a Toyota Prius whose best years are behind it. Accompanied by Marian hymns as sweet as honey, we are on the way to the next largest city. The geographical distance to this city is insignificant. It is much more a temporal distance that we are traveling. When I leave the car again, I will have left behind me over fifty years of Church history and social development. I am on the way to Mass in the form that it used to be celebrated.

And even so, that's how I feel now. It is as if this ramshackle Toyota Prius is a time machine that catapults me back weekly to the 1950s—to a time when female acolytes were just as unacceptable as brotherhood between denominations; to a place where diversity is a foreign word, where everything follows the traditional, Catholic paths, where there is ultimately no place for people like me.

I was born into a Catholic family, became an acolyte, and later wanted to become a priest. At some point, however, I

Queerness IN THE Catholic Church

noticed that I was different. Different from the other boys in my class and, yes, different from what my Church would like to see. At this point, the Latin Mass played no role in my life, and I regularly attended services at my local parish.

It was clear from my family background that I couldn't come out. I decided to become even more Catholic than I already was. I went to church more frequently and prayed the Rosary daily. Eventually I encountered conservative circles and, following that, attended the "Old Mass." I felt good there. The grandeur and the solemnity of the liturgy moved me.

At the same time, this was a place where homosexual people simply couldn't exist because they were not allowed to exist. It was perfect to escape from myself. It was a gift to be able to keep sneaking a glance at the handsome sons of some of the über-Catholics. I was able to hide behind the façade of being a conservative Catholic youth here and no longer had to worry about myself and my sexuality.

This escape from myself went well for a few years. At some point, however, I reached the end of the rope with my Latin. I lost connection with my conservative Catholic parish of choice and, with it, my connection with the Christian faith. I skidded. I left the Church. What followed was an odyssey, but there was no commitment to myself, no yes to my own sexuality.

It would be a few more years before a Catholic priest opened my eyes. He made it clear to me that my homosexuality is not a defect, nothing that I must be ashamed of. Without him, I wouldn't be who I am today. I would have probably kept hiding from myself and my fears. Sometimes there are these people that God sends to you. This priest was and is such a person for me.

Meanwhile, I have been happily married to a man for several years, and I am involved in the Protestant Church as

I Hid behind the Façade of Conservative Catholicism

a predicant, that is, a preacher. I hold services that have absolutely nothing to do with what I experienced in my youth, and I preach a God who has little to do with the god that was preached to me in my childhood and youth. A God who loves us people, no matter who we love.

Memories — Speechlessness — Dreams/Spaces of Faith[1]

Marian Antoni
(born in 1992, student and employee of a
spiritual center for youth)

I feel like a stranger in my own body. Every fiber of my being cried out when I was addressed as "woman"; it reminded me of the seemingly insurmountable compulsion of having to subject myself to a classification throughout my life in which I would never feel at home.

For countless days and nights, I occupied myself with the question of which life corresponds to me best. My intense search and struggle for the right path brought me to a growing realization: it's about me as a whole person, about the opportunity to express myself and live my life in a way that allows me to look in the mirror and recognize myself in it.

In conversations with friends, family members, and pastors, I found more and more language, courage, and trust to take my first, tentative steps. Then, with every day and every

---

1. *Glaubens(t)räume*: the parenthetical "t" changes "faith spaces" to "faith dreams."

Memories—Speechlessness—Dreams/Spaces of Faith

new step, the certainty grew that I had chosen the right path—and was becoming more of who I had always been.

As a person connected to the Church through youth work and as a theology student, I could not avoid dealing with the attitudes of the Church's magisterium during this process. This is unfortunate because, from my perspective, regarding the topic of trans people, the current strategies harbor an enormous potential for injury for those trans people who are religious and Church-affiliated.

The shape of Church society is closely intertwined with a purely binary gender anthropology and cis-heteronormative worldview, which, in relation to trans people, has the effect of radically rejecting this lived reality. Ultimately, the corresponding statements by the magisterial authorities on the subject are so far removed from the actual lived environment and significant experiences of trans people that they remain, at best, irrelevant for those people. At worst, negative statements trigger painful experiences for those addressed when they struggle to integrate their own life path into the realm of faith.

Based on my own biography, it is evident that community engagement in the Church, lived faith, joy in theology, and my trans background form integral parts of my life. Despite deeply hurtful experiences and shocks to my image of the Church, I am still convinced that the institution can learn from direct contact and encounters with trans people and their own questions of faith and life as a matter of course through direct contacts and encounters.

A liberating distancing and (self-)critical reflection on traditional anthropological assumptions not only accords with the demands of academic theology; in view of the global destinies of trans people, the Church has an unavoidable responsibility not to give space to fears, phobias, pathologization, and discrimination that ultimately result in violence, persecution, and the murder of these people.

Queerness IN THE Catholic Church

The traditional biblical narratives and the tradition(s) of Christianity contain a wealth of ambiguous images and diverse life plans. They are testimonies of the transformational potential of God-seeking and faithful people. From my perspective, it therefore seems obvious: spaces of faith are available to all people—especially to those who are in processes of change and becoming or who are concretely faced with life-changing decisions about transitioning.

God Created Me the Way I Am

Charlotte Baron
(born in 2002, volunteer)

As a child, I grew up in a mixed-denomination household and my faith in God and my connection to the Church were primarily exemplified by my Catholic mother. Indeed, I gradually disassociated myself from my own church between the ages of eight and twelve due to a lack of youth ministry. But around the same time, I found a completely new kind of Church home through the youth ministry of the Jesuits at my school. For example, we were allowed to help organize worship services there and occasionally even celebrated Mass outside.

During my teenage years, after long periods of questioning with my closest friends and nuclear family, I came out as bisexual. The reactions were mostly positive, or at least neutral.

In Church contexts and in dealing with Church officials, however, I felt increasingly uncomfortable because of my sexuality. The official sexual morality and the public stance of the Catholic Church also reinforced this feeling. Although very few people I personally dealt with commented on issues concerning LGBTQIA+, the position of women in the Church, or Church sexual morals, I could not be sure of their position on these matters. I didn't know if there were people among them who not only had a different opinion from mine—which wouldn't be wrong—but who would also deny my own sexuality or my love of God.

Therefore, Church settings where these topics are not openly discussed were and are unsafe for me. For me, the Church can only be a truly "safe space," a place where peace, charity, and community can be found, if it takes a stand against misanthropic and marginalizing views.

Due to this lack of a sense of security in Church contexts, my faith has largely decoupled itself from the Church as an institution. While I'm glad that my faith has stayed with me, I still wish to one day feel at home in a Church again, because I am convinced that our own belief in God can become stronger and more crisis-proof when we live it in community with other people.

And I have hope: I have met so many people in the Church who break with convention and welcome people unconditionally! And so, I firmly believe that the Catholic Church can be that community. I remember my former principal giving an Easter sermon on the verse from the creation story: "God saw that it was good" (Gen 1:25). He said, "God created you; he looks at you, and he sees that you are good, just the way you are." This message carries me.

I Am Gay and Catholic—So What?

Jan Baumann
(born in 1991, nurse)

As a child, going to Mass was the highlight of the week for me. Often, I was the driving force behind the motivation for my whole family to go to Sunday Mass. I come from a village of three hundred souls in the Westerwald. Traditions such as village and parish festivals, fairs, community life, and so on are maintained to this day, although these have also declined.

After my first communion, I finally became an altar boy. It was already clear in kindergarten: I wanted to be a priest! A few people in my surroundings informed me about the severe restrictions that this vocation would impose. But when I was still a child, these conditions did not play a role for me.

I ended my altar boy service at the age of seventeen because I switched from the altar to the organ bench. To this day I am a part-time church musician.

During my adolescence, the desire to become a priest gradually faded into the background, mainly because of celibacy. I didn't admit to myself at the time that I was gay. Homosexuality was never seriously talked about in school, in church, or in my family. "Gay" was strictly an insult in the schoolyard. I too was often insulted by it. And who wants to become a living insult?

As I became older, however, my sexual orientation became stronger. At the age of about twenty-one, I decided to finally accept my homosexuality — contrary to village customs and Church doctrine.

I first came out to my sister and my mother, who both took it well. Then came a long period of reflection and the first real and painful confrontation with the Church's doctrine on homosexuality.

After I took part in World Youth Day in Rio de Janeiro in 2013, there was a period in which I believed I could still run away from my homosexuality. I dug out my earlier career aspirations of becoming a priest. My faith was so important to me that it was a liberating thought to be able to escape into this profession. With deceptive enthusiasm, I told a priest, whom I am still friends with today, about my career aspirations that I had felt called to since my childhood. The priest spoke to me very openly and respectfully about the different forms of sexuality and celibacy. After our intense conversation, the hope grew in me that I could belong to and help shape the Church, regardless of my sexuality, but without becoming a priest and becoming celibate.

In another conversation, I came out to that priest. He also took it well. A period of accepting my homosexuality then began. Today, I live with my partner in Münster in Westphalia, where I am fortunate in helping to shape the life of the local queer community. This is a subgroup of the parish of St. Joseph in South Münster that reconciles both being queer and being a Christian — in my case, being gay and Catholic.

With my involvement in the queer community, I would like to help young people shorten the period of inner turmoil I similarly went through, if not spare them from it altogether. I want to show them that being queer and being a Christian are not mutually exclusive. And I want to build bridges to people who are about to give up because of the official Church attitude toward queer people.

How I Met God as a Gay Scientist

Dr. Arturo Blázquez Navarro
(born in 1989, data scientist)

I'm gay, I'm a scientist, I'm Catholic—and I study Catholic theology. "Why are you Catholic? You're a scientist—and you're gay?!" These questions are part of my everyday life. What's more, these questions are a constitutive part of my experience of God. My engagement with theology is my attempt to understand myself and my own life.

Since my early youth, I have been interested in men instead of women. I wasn't able to recognize my homosexuality until I was sixteen, however. I solved the contradiction with Church teaching with the almost clichéd quote from the First Epistle of John: "God is love" (1 John 4:16)! But if God is love, then love must be ordered. At the time, my beliefs were purely conventional. I was just trying to do what was expected of a good boy.

I departed from my faith during this time of studying. That was when I had my first experience of love. I was so filled with happiness that I could hardly comprehend it. In doing so, I realized that this happiness was exactly what I had always expected from faith but had never experienced. I followed that conclusion and became an atheist.

The turning point came in 2015. I was already living in Berlin and was in the middle of preparing for my wedding. It was Good Friday. For weeks, I had felt a deep desire to go to church: "I had a feeling of safety there." Being a good scientist, I tried to explain this phenomenon purely psychologically. In the church, during the veneration of the cross within the Good Friday liturgy, I was unexpectedly struck by a feeling: in the stillness of the veneration of the cross, I met God for the first time.

This original experience has accompanied me ever since. I no longer needed proof of the existence of God because I encountered him in my life. My biography has become a kind of divine empiricism for me. In other words, there is a tiny area within me that is supported by the conviction that I have met God. And whenever I feel emptiness, fear, or despair, I can fall back on it.

As a result, I felt a need to express my gratitude to God. I had many things to be grateful for: my religious experience, but also for my life, my work, and my marriage. At the same time, I felt pressure to justify myself: my marriage and life path within the Church. My response to that pressure was to study theology. I do this as a hobby, however, because I know that, as a married gay Catholic, I will never have the chance to work full time for the Church.

My demands on myself are much more modest: I want to tell other people about God in my everyday life; I want to advocate openly more humanity in the Church. If, at the end of my life, I have even helped one single person come to a faith the size of a mustard seed in this way, then it will have been worth it.

How the Church Makes Life Difficult for My Wife

Anonymous
(born in 1985, digital humanist)

As a nonbeliever, I used to have very little personal contact with the Catholic Church. Above all, I knew the official attitude, with values and positions strongly opposed to my own. The Catholic Church, for me, was synonymous with homophobia, misogyny, and backward-looking, toxic sexual morals. In my eyes, the Church was an oppressive place built on fear and punishment, where charity is preached, but people who live and think differently would be systematically condemned, marginalized, and sometimes actively attacked.

It wasn't until I met my Catholic partner four years ago that a slightly more positive picture was presented to me. I suddenly got to know many people who, for religious reasons, were committed to environmental protection, refugees, and fair trade, who were much more cosmopolitan, tolerant, inclusive, and philanthropic than I had ever expected.

This unexpected openness manifested itself particularly in their very personal attitudes toward the topics of love and

How the Church Makes Life Difficult for My Wife

sexuality, especially homosexuality, premarital sex, and celibacy, but especially toward (gender) identity and the role of women and men in Church and society. I began to revise my view of the Church and see the individual people—separate from the institution.

But I increasingly observed that the people who provided me with this apparently modern picture of the Catholic Church always either put themselves in a cautiously relativistic position or even very explicitly and consciously opposed the official position of the Church with their actions and attitudes. They weren't exactly people who would be considered "good" or "proper" Catholics.

At the same time, I have witnessed people calling my partner a sinner and asking her to deny her identity, invoking the Church's official, conservative sexual morality. I saw how much she was suffering. Because of her relationship with me, she suddenly no longer seemed welcome in the Church where she had once felt so comfortable.

My partner's relationship with her strict Catholic family, with whom she had previously had a normal, loving relationship, was suddenly severely strained. At times, it seemed as if she would be expelled not only from the Church but also from her family. The situation has since calmed down. They now act as if this relationship does not exist at all.

My wish for my partner is that the openness and tolerance of the believers I have met would also be reflected in the official attitude of the Catholic Church and that families would no longer be forced to choose between their Church and their daughter, granddaughter, or sister.

Finding the Strength to Come Out

Anonymous
(born in 1990, civil service employee)

I realized very early on in my life that I was gay. Shortly after puberty, I began to have this tingling in my stomach when thinking about some classmates. Nevertheless, a good ten years full of doubts went by before I came out. The fear of not being accepted kept growing. The reactions from my personal environment after my coming out were, however, so positive that I will never forget these moments. Since then, whenever anyone has asked me about it, I am open about my homosexuality. I don't force knowledge of my sexual orientation on anyone, though, because it's just a part of my personality.

For me, being gay doesn't mean that I must surround myself only with other LGBTQIA+ people. Even as a gay person, I can have an ordinary circle of friends in which sexual orientation does not play a role. My contacts with the LGBTQIA+ community are therefore limited to a few make-outs at Oktoberfest and a few more intense touches. I haven't had a steady relationship yet.

Faith plays a big role for me personally. To this day, I pray the prayers I learned from my grandmother every night

Finding the Strength to Come Out

before I go to bed. I was raised as a Christian and was involved in Church life from the start. My commitment is not limited to the work in the parish but also extends to voluntary work in the deanery and the diocese. I feel that I am accepted as I am and don't have to pretend, especially in the youth work of the Young Catholic Community (KjG).[1] This community motivated me to open up to others. I received the needed strength to do so in this community and might still not be out today without it.

For me, there is a big difference between the official Church and the faithful. I have a troubled relationship with the official Church. Personally, however, the faithful make up the real Church and community. I have met with encouragement and acceptance almost without exception in my parish and the KjG. That's why I'm still very happy to be active within it on a voluntary basis.

My wish is that the Church would not make a distinction between heterosexual and homosexual love. I don't want special treatment. I just want to live a normal life in the comfort of marriage and family. I didn't choose to be gay. I'm not doing this out of any ideology or out of protest but simply because I am. While I would be very sad if the official Church did not move on its views on homosexuality, I know deep down that God loves me just the way I am and that he would never judge me for my sexual orientation. And I'm absolutely convinced of that. That's why I will continue to live my faith and pass on my convictions.

---

1. *Katholische junge Gemeinde*, lit. "Young Catholic Community"; an important German Catholic youth organization that leans to the more progressive side theologically and politically. They encourage kids, teens, and young adults to get involved actively and act politically. See www.kjg.de for more information.

Catholic Means Universal and That Includes Everyone

Verena Eitzenberger
(born in 1936, retiree)

One morning after the worship service, a young man stood in front of our church somewhat lost. I had never seen him before. He seemed lonely and depressed. I asked him who he was and where he came from. He answered evasively. When I asked where he was going now, he didn't know what to say. I asked him if he had already had breakfast. He said no. So I invited him to my house and had breakfast with him. He was very taciturn but had an enormous appetite. When we parted, I asked him if he would like to come again. "Yes, gladly," he answered.

Since then, he has often been my guest. Over time, I learned that life is not easy for him. I didn't find out at first that he was gay. I only found out about this much later, by chance. Until then, I had never spent time with anyone who wasn't straight—at least not that I knew of. I knew there were people who were not heterosexual, but they had never come into my life. It was immediately clear to me, however, that it

Catholic Means Universal and That Includes Everyone

didn't matter to me whether that young man was gay or whatever. He was important to me as a person.

It was the Catholic faith that helped me. I know the Church's position on homosexuality and homosexual people, but for me the most important commandment of the Christian faith is charity. I grew up with this belief; I have lived my whole life with this belief. The theses-posting of Mary 2.0 on February 21, 2021,[1] in which I took part myself, and the #lovewins campaign on May 9 and 10, 2021,[2] which I followed closely, made me realize for the first time how badly gay and other non-straight people are treated by the Church.

Since then, I've met quite a few nonheterosexual people—people I've found to be deeply religious and extremely sensitive. I don't think anyone has a right to put themselves above these people, let alone treat them as second-class citizens. This should be the case even more in a Church that upholds the standard of the commandment to love one's neighbor. A rethinking is needed in the Catholic Church—a rethinking

---

1. Mary 2.0 (*Maria 2.0*) is a movement in Germany that began in 2019. They advocate for the full inclusion of women in ministry, an end to clerical celibacy, a more "colorful" appreciation and recognition of realistic sexual morality, and a civil reckoning for clergy accused of sexual abuse. They have often held Masses outside of churches to make their views known. On February 21, 2021, supporters from all over Germany re-created Martin Luther's posting of the *Ninety-Five Theses* by posting the seven theses of the Mary 2.0 movement. For more information see www.mariazweipunktnull.de.

2. See Congregation for the Doctrine of the Faith, *Responsum of the Congregation for the Doctrine of the Faith to a Dubium regarding the Blessing of the Unions of Persons of the Same Sex* (March 15, 2021). The Vatican responded to a question regarding the blessing of same-sex unions by saying that God "does not and cannot bless sin," effectively banning priests from blessing any same-sex relationship. In response, several German priests held blessing ceremonies on May 9 and 10, 2021, publicized with the hashtag #liebegewinnt (love wins). See Rudolf Gehring, "Widerstand Gegen 'Nein' Des Vatikan: Segnungsfeiern Bei 'Aktionstag' in Deutschen Kirchen," CNA-deutsch, Catholic News Agency, May 10, 2021, https://de.catholicnewsagency.com/story/bundesweite-protestaktion-aktivisten-spenden-segen-fuer-homosexuelle-paare-8404.

toward an attitude that puts people at the center, regardless of how God created them.

I belong to a generation in which such topics were taboo for a long time. And what wasn't talked about didn't seem to exist either. So I understand that many people of my generation find it difficult to accept that there are nonheterosexual people and that they have the same rights as everyone else. But I also know from my own experience that you are never too old to learn new things and to rethink things. This also applies to the Church. And that's why I'm not giving up hope that, one day, the Catholic Church will be what it claims to be: Catholic. *Catholic* means universal and that includes everyone.

The Beam in the Eye

Dr. Johannes zu Eltz
(born in 1957, priest, pastor, and canon)

My first encounter with the subject of "queer and Catholic" took place at the College of St. Blasien in the Black Forest, where I attended boarding school from 1967 to 1976. In the boys' and men's world of the college, the comment, "You gay pig!" was quickly blurted out in an argument as a broad-spectrum, nonspecific insult. If someone was seriously suspected of homosexual tendencies, however, he had nothing to laugh about. Not being normal, cool, not belonging. Exclusion from the community brought social death.

I don't recall the Jesuits or other teaching and educational staff saying a word about sexual integration and identity issues. We were left to ourselves and each other. The indifference of leadership and the reinforcing of the violent and fear-ridden field with massive taboos ensured that sexuality was not an issue. This was not the worst thing under the given conditions, I think to myself now with fifty years of distance. But a friendly reminder around adolescence that sexual orientation, like everything else in human beings, grows gradually and does not fall out of the sky, and that God loves everyone just as they are—that would have saved me a lot of fear and heartache. For a long time, these took away my joy in myself and my spontaneity in dealing with others.

Queerness IN THE Catholic Church

The next encounter was in Frankfurt in 2010. When I became city dean there, the "Project: Gay and Catholic in the Parish of Our Lady Help of Christians"[1] fell at my feet. In an interview that appeared as a foreword in the German-language edition of the bestseller *Building a Bridge* by Fr. James Martin, SJ, I explained why, contrary to expectations, I did not take offense at this but thought it to be a cornerstone for the new outreach of the town church.

By that time, I had already been a priest for twenty years and had come to terms with the contradictions of Church teaching and practice over the years. I not only endured them passively but actively supported them. English knows the pair of opposites "allowing—forbidding" as a human attitude, untranslatable into German. I've talked about homosexuality and homosexuals so "forbiddingly" that no one has ever come to me for confidence, for advice, or for help.

"Where is the problem?" I thought. The problem was within me, I know now, and it is within the Catholic Church. It is the proverbial beam in your own eye that severely limits your field of vision. Not a good prerequisite for "see–judge–act."

I see many priests with "deep-seated homosexual tendencies,"[2] which, by canon law, should not exist. The Church willingly keeps them, and many of them unwillingly hold the Church hostage in its condemnation of homosexuality. This is a grand clerical delusion and, in my judgment, a structural sin. Surely, God can forgive us, but active repentance must precede it: a doctrinal revision that learns from human science and is resolutely directed toward the salvation of souls.

---

1. *Projekt: schwul und katholisch in [der Gemeinde] Maria Hilf (PSK)* is a noncanonical personal parish in Frankfurt in Main, which welcomes LGBTQIA+ Catholics.
2. Congregation for Catholic Education, "Instruction Concerning the Criteria for the Discernment of Vocations with regard to Persons with Homosexual Tendencies in View of Their Admission to the Seminary and to Holy Orders," November 4, 2005.

Closest Loves Like Yourself

Johannes Engelhardt
(born in 1959, restaurant owner)

My relationship with the Catholic Church has cooled off a lot for a long time. I've given up hope that people who want to reform it with a liberal, grounded, democratic attitude can make a difference. You can't turn an old fortress into a light-flooded, modern house. To stay with the metaphor: rather than preserving the castle like a museum, erecting a bold new building would probably be more expedient.

Growing up in a rural environment, I was spiritually shaped by my mother's sincere folk beliefs and my grandmother's unspoken godly devotion. As a child, I never questioned going to church on Sundays. I never liked it. I didn't understand what the pastor, who used to pull us up by the hairline above the ear when we misbehaved in religion class, was saying. I often got sick from the incense, and the worst part was that I wasn't allowed to sit next to my friend Helga. In those days, boys and girls had separate seats in the service. Later, I had a catechist in religion class. If she wanted to punish you, you had to make a fist, and she then pounded your

Queerness IN THE Catholic Church

knuckles over the edge of the table. No wonder that as a child I was more afraid and terrified of anything Catholic.

My coming out to my parents and friends was either not taken seriously or met with denial. It broke up my family. I knew the Catholic Church had a problem with my being gay. Nevertheless, in my desperation and forlornness at the time, I also looked to it for help. I did not find this help. So, I left the Church when I was eighteen.

I didn't want to have anything to do with an institution that didn't want to take me for who I am. Over time, I fell in love, had a relationship, and got involved in a center for queer people. This process of emancipation lasted a long time, until my thirties. I was lucky. Today, I am married and can live my life undisguised. I very much hope that LGBTQIA+ young people will now be able to discover themselves faster and with less pain.

The question of faith—that is, of the existential things in life—accompanies me to this day. I have found my spiritual point of view—one that is not tied to any institution. In my more than twenty years of work as a hospice volunteer, I have experienced again and again that the really important things in life are simply about one thing: trusting that our limited, imperfect existence is correct and that it can comfort us in an emergency.

The attitude of the Catholic Church toward LGBTQIA+ people and its failure to deal with the abuse cases stuns and saddens me. But I am also saddened by the realization of how wholesome and beneficial the Catholic Church could be if it kept at least this one commandment: "You shall love your neighbor as yourself" (Lev 19:18).

Examination of Conscience

Lukas Färber
(born in 1998, parish youth minister and student)

My friends often ask me, without understanding, why I volunteer and work for an organization that discriminates against me as a man who loves other men. I then tell them about the wonderful experiences I had in the youth organizations, about the great people I was able to meet, about the important work that is done through Church organizations. With each subsequent story, it feels more and more like a half-hearted justification, a story I must tell myself to avoid losing my Church home. If I'm honest with myself, I rarely try to convince my interlocuter with these justifications. Rather, I must convince my own conscience for supporting an unjust system like the Catholic Church with my time and energy.

Since my youth I have been passionately involved in various Catholic youth organizations, primarily as diocesan leader in the Young Catholic Community (KjG) in the Diocese of Münster. For me, this community is a place where the focus is the core of our gospel and living this out in a contemporary way. The message of liberation, justice, and love that Jesus brought to our world permeates the work of the associations at

Queerness IN THE Catholic Church

all levels—the group lessons and summer camps, the work of the boards and committees, as well as the political advocacy work. Grounded in this message, young people become active and fight for gender equality and for the rights of LGBTQIA+ people in the Church and in society, among other things. In associations such as the KjG, important safe spaces are created for queer people who want to live their faith in community despite the anti-LGBTQIA+ teachings of the Catholic Church—safe spaces for people like me. It is there that I gathered the self-confidence and trust in God*[1] to stand by me. I still gather strength and energy there today when I express my sadness, my anger, and my horror in the spiritual battle for a just and nondiscriminatory Church.

But my conscience keeps knocking on my door to remind me that with all the positive things that Church associations, organizations, and many laypeople do in parishes, the local church is always supported by the official Church. This official Church conceals violence, does not recognize the universal and inviolable dignity of all people, and discriminates against me and countless others. My justifications still work for me; there is still hope—even if only a weak one—that discrimination can be overcome. I now admit to myself that I don't know how long it will stay like this; that I don't know when I'll have to give up my Church home to save my faith. But even if my Church does, my God* does not discriminate—and this certainty remains.

---

1. *Gott* vertrauen.* The asterisk (*Genderstelle,* "gender-star") indicates a genderless form of the noun, "God," in German.

Why Are We Still Catholic as a Rainbow Family?

Ulrike Fasching
(born in 1970, architect)

I have good memories of my school days in a state-recognized, Dominican girls' high school in Munich. In the 1980s, in addition to the lay teachers, seven sisters worked there as teachers, as well as a religion teacher from the Dominican order. The atmosphere was relaxed and pleasant. We felt accepted there, as different as we all were. I experienced predominantly liberal-minded teachers, especially the sisters, who exemplified social- and value-oriented relationships and tolerance. I remember my Catholic religion teacher teaching us that only all religions together could reflect the true and whole image of God—a construct of ideas, feelings, and associations.

For some time and to the present, many Catholics live in a different reality, even a kind of parallel world, from that of the faith and morals proclaimed by the institutional Church. The division is widening; the need for reform is obvious. Sometimes we, as a rainbow family (i.e., a family parented by two people of the same sex), are asked why we are still members of the Catholic Church. The question always sounds like we are prone to self-hating behavior.

It is the small interpersonal experiences that give us hope for change, that show that at least some Catholic clergy understand and live the Christian message differently. We had an intense and beautiful experience on the evening of our civil wedding when our friend, a deacon, blessed both our relationship and our unborn son in the womb.

But the blessing ceremonies in spring 2021 in Germany have also shown that many Catholic clergy also want to enforce the basic and human rights guaranteed in the German constitution for LGBTQIA+ people in the Church. They are committed to the acceptance and blessing of same-sex couples. In doing so, they opposed the recently published paper from Rome banning the blessing of couples. Those who do it anyway are brave! Change can succeed only when it comes from within.

The "Gay Lobby" in the Vatican — Fact or Fiction?

Ingo-Michael Feth
(born in 1966, journalist)

To get straight to the point: I will disappoint anyone who expects a revenge piece with the Catholic Church in this chapter. I suffer neither from mental damage nor from repressed trauma caused by my Catholic baptismal certificate. In addition, I still belong to the Catholic Church and would describe myself as a believer, if asked.

The numerous scandals, some annoying Vatican documents, ossified structures, lukewarm ground staff, and other diverse shortcomings have not been able to change anything. Maybe I just got lucky. For example, there were three clergymen who accompanied me in my childhood, youth, and as a young adult, even leading me to the threshold of entering the seminary, where I very seriously believed my vocation stood.

I didn't become a priest; I became a journalist. In a way, both have to do with the "power of the word." Some people might now say: "Aha, then his disposition probably prevented him from becoming a priest." The answer is a clear no. Even

Queerness IN THE Catholic Church

then it was crystal clear to me that there were many like me in the seminary. You didn't even have to play hide-and-seek; it was rather liberal there.

The Archdiocese of Munich and Freising was by no means a conservative bulwark during the long tenure of Friedrich Cardinal Wetter. The first official AIDS pastoral ministry of any German dioceses was introduced in Munich in 1990; Cardinal Wetter personally inaugurated the spaces in Schwabing. The pastoral reality had long since said goodbye to iron dogma.

When I went to the sacristy in St. Michael's after the late-evening Mass, which my partner and I liked to attend, to thank the celebrant for his refreshing sermon, he invited me to spend the whole evening discussing everything about God and the world—nothing was off limits.

I have been living and working in Rome for eight years now. The universal Church up close! After several world synods of bishops, papal teachings, Vatileaks, and various commotions about an alleged "gay lobby" in the Vatican, I can say one thing today: Rome simply works differently from how most German Catholics imagine. And I don't necessarily mean that in a negative way. "The world Church should recover from the German character"[1]—it doesn't work that way.

What we take for granted in the enlightened West— marriage for all—is beyond imagination in other parts of the world. Even Pope Francis is in a quandary, since as Pontifex Maximus, he has to protect the unity of the Church. My conclusion as a journalistic observer: A Vatican document that

---

1. An inversion of a quote from the Bishop of Augsburg, Dr. Bertram Meier, "Am deutschen Wesen wird die Weltkirche sicher nicht genesen," in Thorsten Paprotny, "Am Deutschen Wesen Wird Die Weltkirche Nicht Genesen," CNA Deutsch, Catholic News Agency, October 23, 2021, https://de.catholicnewsagency.com/article/am-deutschen-wesen-wird-die-weltkirche-nicht-genesen-1526.

The "Gay Lobby" in the Vatican—Fact or Fiction?

officially recognizes homosexual partnerships is no longer to be expected, at least in this pontificate.

When my gay novel, *Confiteor—I Confess*, set in the Vatican, was published in 2007, it was still considered daring and even scandalous. Reality has now overtaken fiction. Some time ago, I dined with a high curial prelate, casually mentioning my book. My counterpart looked at me with wide eyes, then burst out laughing: "You're the author? Crazy! Your novel was passed around enthusiastically here in the Vatican. You have to sign my copy for me." Since then, I've been wondering: Is my Vatican readership the infamous "gay lobby" that has been the subject of so much speculation?

Confiteor — Convertere

Joachim Frank
(born in 1965, journalist)

Confiteor. Mea culpa. "I confess. My guilt." Perhaps it is good for a person used to fiery antidiscrimination speeches and appeals for equal rights from Catholic decision-makers to recall one's own history of mental and habitual guilt. A history of prejudice, thoughtlessness, and contradictions in dealing with homosexual people.

I brought with me, from my childhood home, an instilled alienation in which "civility and morality" were more dominant than Catholic morality. Luckily in my parents' house, I was spared from supposedly pious figures of speech such as "Anyone who does such things is an abomination to the Lord." But the conviction that "homos are not normal" was unquestioned.

Based on this ready-made system of coordinates, it was clear who was on the right side and who was on the wrong side, even while studying theology. And how funny were the shamefully childish pranks that were played on a fellow student who danced ballet. His special underpants with testicle protection had disappeared without a trace from the laundry room.

I was pleasantly shocked during discussions with seminary professors and spiritual directors about the high proportion of homosexuals in the clergy. When a fellow student came out and resigned from his priestly training, things I hadn't noticed during my own training started to become clearer. I had been blind to the obvious, a knot in my brain, and chain-mail around my heart.

The news brought a moment of terror: A prominent cleric from the Münster diocese disappeared, almost overnight—"because of a man." But that wasn't what pissed me off. Rather, it was the fact that the same minister was earlier known and feared as a "gay hunter."

I could tell stories like this of split realities and double standards in abundance. I should perhaps mention the dictum of Cologne's Joachim Cardinal Meisner: that he never laid his hands on any homosexuals in consecration. Again and again, this was an occasion for mocking laughter that should have got stuck in one's throat or, better, led to frank discussions in the service of truth and truthfulness.

It is not a long way to go from statements like Meisner's to the denial of reality by the magisterium that, in its frost-bitten brutality, must also cause pain to heterosexual people. Only a few months after his papal election in 2005, Benedict XVI approved an instruction for the Roman Congregation for Catholic Education.[1] It forbids the ordination of men with "deep-seated homosexual tendencies" because they are "gravely hindered" from "relating correctly to men and women."

The magisterium has erected a building of lies through their hubris, scientific ignorance, and perversion (in the literal sense: twisting) of reality: a Church-based prison of thought, speech, and acting in the spirit of Jesus. It is high time that this

---

1. "Instruction Concerning the Criteria for the Discernment of Vocations with regard to Persons with Homosexual Tendencies in View of Their Admission to the Seminary and to Holy Order," https://www.vatican.va/roman_curia/congregations/ccatheduc/documents/rc_con_ccatheduc_doc_20051104_istruzione_en.html.

prison was demolished, not least of all because of the obvious, fatal consequences of such imprisonment—the abuse scandal.

But something else has also become apparent: the point at which loyalty to one's own Church turns into complicity. Standing in front of this "point of no return," the *Confiteor* must become an accusation with an *accuso* at the beginning and a call to repentance with a *convertete!* at the end.

How a Selfie with "Prince Charming" Changed My Life

Henry Frömmichen
(born in 1999, funeral director)

Even as a child, I was enthusiastic about the Christian faith and was involved in a variety of ways in my Church community. It soon became clear to me that I wanted to become a Catholic priest. My home pastor at the time was my role model. He recognized my enthusiasm and passion for Church and faith in my third-grade religious education class and accepted me with care and benevolence.

At the age of sixteen, I was able to come out as a homosexual person. I came out during a pastoral conversation with a priest. His encouragement that God loves me just the way I am gave me great strength and new courage to face life. I had lost both through the time of inner struggle and wrestling with my sexual orientation. I was aware that I could no longer pursue my heart's desire, indeed my vocation, to become a priest because I had now come out as homosexual. But the priest encouraged me and assured me that it doesn't matter even a little what my sexual orientation is; he knows a lot of

Queerness IN THE Catholic Church

gay priests who all do excellent work in their parishes. If I continue to feel the call of the Lord and the fire in me, I should just keep walking this path.

I was released three months after entering the seminary of the Archdiocese of Munich and Freising. In November 2020, I posted a selfie with the main protagonist of the gay reality dating show *Prince Charming*, Alexander Schäfer, on the social media platform Instagram. I wanted to send a signal that even though I intend to become a priest, I will not forget about the people—certainly not those who are discriminated against and marginalized by the Catholic Church because of their sexual orientation or gender identity.

The seminary leaders accused me of showing solidarity with homosexual people and propagating the type and lifestyle of homosexual people as portrayed in the TV series. I am no longer acceptable as a seminarian. I'm not discouraged by this dismissal, however. I continue to fight for an open, Catholic, all-encompassing Church in which everyone is allowed to be who they are and no one is discriminated against or marginalized.

World Church on Site

Dieter Geerlings
(born in 1947, auxiliary bishop emeritus of Münster)

Spring 2021: The rainbow flag is flying at St. Pius Church in Münster. The Catholic youth of the local parish hung it up with the consent of the pastor. The flag flutters as a sign of protest over the Vatican's no to the blessing of homosexual couples. No one considered the fact that this church almost exclusively hosts congregations of other languages: Africans, Arabic-speaking Maronites, a Hungarian congregation. Many of its members cannot make friends with this flag. There was no communication with them before this protest action, which was met with confusion. It is not the way they would demonstrate against a decision from the Vatican. Of course, they don't want to discriminate against people with a different sexual orientation, but their traditions on this are different from some others in the country. The rainbow flag at "their" church bothers them greatly.

The Maronite pastor and the head of the Department of Foreign Language Congregations brought this situation to my attention as the episcopal representative for foreign language congregations. Members of all the congregations named here, the young people, and the pastor agreed to a conversation after a Sunday service.

Queerness IN THE Catholic Church

My attitude to the whole topic is publicly known online and in other media:[1] If people are responsible, willing to commit to a same-sex partnership, and want to live out that commitment, they should receive a blessing from the Church, provided they want one. I cannot see how that can be confused with the sacrament of marriage. Taking responsibility for one another is worthy of blessing. I am skeptical of general blessing ceremonies, as they can lead to trivializing the issue. I understand homosexuality as a "variety of human relationships and the ability to relate" with biogenetic (and other) causes.

It was agreed, however, that the discussion should be about only one thing: What are we going to do with the flag? In the end, there was a mutual agreement to take down the flag. The young people said they were willing to do this, recognizing that they should have communicated with the other congregations beforehand. The young people highly appreciated that the other congregations had respected the flag at the church for weeks, although they have a different opinion on it. They wanted to respond to this tolerant behavior with tolerance of their own. They all agreed to another joint discussion on the subject.

This conversation was very open and clearly made a difference, as can be seen in the statement, "Today, the understanding is growing that the Bible passages that are referred to in Church documents on our subject do not mention what we today understand by same-sex orientation." Such statements led to more discussions about other different cultural contexts or traditions. The conversation will continue.

---

1. Many such articles are in German. For an example in English, see Robert Shine, "German Bishop Reaffirms His Request for Church Blessings and Civil Partnerships for Same-Gender Couples," New Ways Ministry, August 23, 2019, https://www.newwaysministry.org/2019/08/25/german-bishop-reaffirms-his-request-for-church-blessings-and-civil-partnerships-for-same-gender-couples/.

World Church on Site

Being a Christian does not mean holding on to a form of faith bound to one time and culture. Rather, it is about realizing a new living praxis in which the gospel keeps gaining new shape and profile. It is about new life for all people.

Therefore, the flags continue to fly elsewhere….

A Gay Couple in the Church for Five Decades

Manfred Hassemer-Tiedeken
(born in 1950, retired)

I have been living with my husband, Hajo, a former religious, for half a century now. I used to work as a nurse myself. We married civilly in 2009. We met in 1972 through a personal ad in *him*, a magazine for homosexuals.

From the beginning, we have felt very comfortable in our Catholic parishes in our respective places of residence—whether it be Ahlen in Westphalia, Westerland on Sylt, Koblenz, Bremen, Rüdersdorf near Berlin, or Neukölln in Berlin. Our love has never been a problem—neither for our respective ministers[1] nor for our fellow Christians. We always came out in conversations from the start: "We're gay, we vote for the Greens,[2] and one of us pays our Church tax directly to a parish in Peru and not to the official German Church."

---

1. *jeweiligen Seelsorgerinnen und Seelsorger*, both female and male pastoral ministers are explicit in the German.

2. Fully "Alliance 90/The Greens," *Bündnis 90/Die Grünen*, a center-left political party in Germany, similar to the Green party in America and elsewhere.

A Gay Couple in the Church for Five Decades

We were welcomed into all communities and were able to get involved in parish life. We have accompanied confirmands on their way, were elected members of the parish council and church board, and have been involved in Church asylum and homeless work—always as an openly gay couple.

The topic of homosexuality was never a big deal, but it was not kept secret either. We cofounded the group Homosexuals and Church and have been active in it for many years. We organized meetings in church rooms, had lively discussions with visitors at *Katholikentag*,[3] and were able to have fruitful conversations with young men and women before their coming out, with parents and relatives of homosexual people, with bishops and theologians, and even with outspoken homophobes.

We were saddened and angered by the many life stories of people who, because of their sexual orientation, were attacked in the worst possible way by priests, religious, and other representatives of the Catholic Church, who were denied the right to call themselves Catholic, and who, despite many years of active and reliable participation, were marginalized and pushed out of their parishes.

This made us sad and angry, especially because we ourselves have so rarely been denigrated or discriminated against by the Church in all these many years. That's why I still remember a good-natured and pious member of the parish who once expressed to us his regret that we could not go to heaven, since we ended up living in sin, eating "the bread" and drinking "of the cup of the Lord unworthily" thereby incurring "judgment" (see 1 Cor 11:27).

We are glad that within the Catholic Church, at least

---

3. "Catholic Day" occurs every two years in a different city. It is organized by the laity and thus reflects the current social environment. There are worship services, seminars, workshops, concerts, and other opportunities for engagement, education, and entertainment.

in Germany, more understanding and goodwill is gradually developing toward Christians living with the same sex.⁴ Nevertheless, there is still a lot of resistance, but we hope to be able to break through it eventually through conversations and persuasion.

---

4. *gleichgeschlechtlich l(i)ebenden Christen*, the parenthetical "t" changes *lebenden*, "Christians *living* with a same-sex [partner]," to *liebenden*, "Christians *loving* [a person] of the same sex."

God Has a Plan for Me as a Gay Man

Dr. Andreas Helfrich
(born in 1964, architect)

I was born in Speyer and baptized Catholic. Through my parents, my brothers and I were able to experience a Christian upbringing, for which I am very grateful to this day.

Over the course of my life, this socialization has given me stability and strength in moments that were very difficult and seemed hopeless. I met and fell in love with my current partner twenty-six years ago, and twelve years ago, we were married civilly in Cologne.

We have been through thick and thin together over the years. We were and are always there for each other, in good times and bad, especially when the other was sick, couldn't take it anymore, or needed strength and comfort. We have mastered the crises in our partnership together thus far.

How we longed to have God's blessings on this relationship too! In all the years that I have worked as an architect in a management position for a housing project of the Catholic Church in Cologne, I have increasingly experienced how taciturn, how closed off, and how withdrawn I became, even to the point of denying who I was.

Queerness in the Catholic Church

The Catholic Church didn't make it easy for me to accept my own sexuality. It does not encourage people to believe that what one does, what one feels, is part of some great divine plan. God created gay people too. The Catholic Church refuses to recognize this fact.

An elaborate system based on guilt and a strictly repressive sexual morality stand in the way, even within her own ranks.

With a heavy heart, I took the Vatican's unbearable declarations on homosexuality as the ultimate reason to leave the Catholic Church.

In May 2021, one of my brothers made my partner and me aware of the #lovewins campaign,[1] in which many Catholic clergymen nationwide blessed couples who avowed their love in a partnership. We spontaneously went to one of the services in Cologne and received God's blessing. What a wonderful gift!

No institution can deny God's blessing when it comes to love between two people vowed to one another. I am sure that God still has a plan for me as a gay man in this world and in the Christian church today. The #lovewins campaign was a ray of light, a glimmer of hope that I may still have a place in the Church. Maybe there is a way back....

---

1. See "Catholic Means Universal and That Includes Everyone," note 4.

When Two Men Love Each Other, That's Just Love

Markus Helfrich
(born in 1971, personnel manager)

I grew up in a Catholic family and have two older brothers who have had a significant impact on me. Then and now, I always seem to align myself with them. Our parents brought us up in a socially conservative, Catholic way, although as the youngest descendant I certainly experienced the already-waning severity of the late 1970s.

    I have always perceived our parents as caring and loving but also as a moral authority. It wasn't until I was growing up that I understood what influences and experiences our parents had during their childhood and adolescence. Their growing up, adolescence, and starting a family took place in the social context of the late 1930s through to the early 1960s, particularly in a middle-class environment. In this context, homosexuality wasn't something that was talked about openly. It wasn't at all in accordance with the vested and imparted Catholic values; it was even considered criminal.

Queerness IN THE Catholic Church

With this background, the coming out of my middle brother was a bombshell and shook the world of our parents. They wondered how this could have happened: their own son, of all people, a successful, attractive man, more important, a valuable, liberal-minded person, endearing, full of goodness and love....Weeks and months of strife and (doubt and) despair passed.[1] There is no question that their love for their own son was unwavering—and yet our parents had a hard time with it at first.

What happened next made a deep impression on me: through my brother's relationship with his partner, our parents began to question themselves and their own values, but also the values of society and the Church. It seemed as if they didn't want to conform anymore, couldn't conform anymore, and maybe never conformed—never conformed to the reality of two people who love and respect each other and spend their lives together, with all the challenges of such a partnership. No more and no less. How could that not be in God's design? Why shouldn't this fulfill the message of Jesus?

My brother's partner became a permanent member of our family over time, and the later civil union between the two became a family celebration. The gay couple in the middle of our family has become what it is and what it should be: it has become normalized, without classification, without special status, without ifs and buts.

Today, when I see my father hugging my brother's partner—my best man and brother-in-law—and how happy he is when they see them both make vacation plans together, I'm just proud, proud of my parents and their ability to support each other in their old age through their questioning processes, discarding conventions and opening up, out of love,

---

1. *(Ver-)Zweifelns. Verzweifelns* is "despair" and *Zweifelns* is "doubt."

When Two Men Love Each Other, That's Just Love

but also out of hard-earned, worked-for conviction. They will always be role models for me.

I sincerely wish for our Church to go through this process as well. It is certainly not an easy process. But anyone who preaches the love of God, who represents the messages of Jesus Christ, and who wants to convey the message of Jesus Christ credibly and sincerely to people must question themselves, doubt old beliefs, ask themselves questions about their own history, and face reality. Because this reality is nothing more than the love of two people—nothing more and nothing less.

A Gay Man Opened My Door to the Church

Simone Hock
(born in 1974, office clerk)

I was born in what was then the GDR[1] and was baptized as a Protestant when I was a small child. I was not, however, brought up in the faith—on the contrary, in line with the socialist image of humanity in the GDR and its state party, the *SED*,[2] I became a convinced atheist. Believe in God? That's something for the weak, for people who don't want to take responsibility for their lives, not for an intelligent, enlightened person of today.

Nevertheless, films and books based on biblical stories have always held a special fascination for me. The fact that I am a member of the Catholic Church today has a lot to do with a gay man. I got to know Wolfgang professionally in 2016; privately we met again in our city's Democratic Alliance. Mutual sympathies eventually led to an invitation to dinner with him and his life partner. That was on April 12, 2017, the Wednes-

---

1. The German Democratic Republic (*Deutsche Demokratische Republik*), commonly, East Germany.
2. The Socialist Unity Party of Germany (*Sozialistische Einheitspartei Deutschlands*), commonly, the East German Communist Party.

A Gay Man Opened My Door to the Church

day of Holy Week. The unfinished Easter candle stood on the table and I, as a member of the Left Party,[3] was teased that the communist could now help to finish the Easter candle. Later Wolfgang enthusiastically spoke about the Easter Vigil in his parish church.

Many conversations about God followed. They just happened naturally because Wolfgang lives his faith naturally. Because I was baptized a Protestant, he first attended Protestant services with me—I didn't dare to go alone—and at the first service, baptismal promises were renewed. A very touching moment. Nevertheless, I always left Protestant services feeling that they were missing a little something. That changed when I first attended Mass in Wolfgang's parish church in November 2017. I knew immediately that this is where I belong. In February 2018, I contacted the pastor, and, in October 2018, I was accepted into the Catholic Church and confirmed. And of course, Wolfgang, now my best friend, was also my sponsor.

In March 2019, I was elected to the Catholic Council of my diocese and that same year, Wolfgang and his husband got married after being together for twelve years. The church wedding, the blessing ceremony, was very special, and I was allowed to be the wedding photographer. The Protestant pastor said, "We are not blessing your love and life together, but that you are bringing your love before God." As touching as the whole celebration was, it also made me sad. It was not only missing a Catholic priest, but the blessing from both denominations would have been good. That was the question: Why shouldn't one bless the love of two people and their journey through life together?

God gave us love. He gave us his unlimited love, for we are all made in his image, including our sexuality. He gave

---

3. *DIE LINKE*, lit. "The Left." A democratic-socialist, far-left German political party.

Queerness IN THE Catholic Church

us love to give it to him, and to feel it for one another, to love nature and the environment, animals, music, culture—love in so many different forms. And I ask myself: Why not bless the love of two people and their journey through life together? Can God do anything greater than joining two people together and uniting them in love? So why not bless what God has joined together?

A same-sex couple was baptized in my church in June 2021. A trans woman from the neighboring congregation comes to our service because she was attacked for being different by strangers from her parish while on her way to the church. She no longer feels safe there. Whenever the issue comes up, or whenever I need to bring it up, I promote acceptance and blessing of different life plans.

For a Long Time, I Felt My Homosexuality Was a Sin and Shame

Giovanni Inzerilli
(born in 1972, certified nursing assistant)

Having been born in Sicily, the Catholic faith has always been a very important part of my life. There, in my homeland, services, processions, and other religious celebrations are constantly taking place. The Catholic faith is a matter of course for all generations. The attitude of most people there is rather conservative accordingly.

I grew up in poverty, and as a child I had a very close relationship with God. To refresh my baptism, I often went to church and secretly poured holy water over my head. Afterward, I always felt reborn and full of strength. When I picked flowers, I always brought half to my mother and half to church. The commandments and rules of the Catholic Church have always been authoritative for me; I never questioned what our pastor said.

It quickly became clear during adolescence that I was homosexual. I was ashamed of it. That's why I couldn't tell anyone about it. I had to hide my feelings. I couldn't even

Queerness IN THE Catholic Church

talk about it in confession, although I felt my sexuality to be a serious sin.

At the age of twenty-four, I came to Germany with nothing but a little coffee. It was easier for me here. Homosexuality was not kept under wraps like in Sicily and homosexuals were less marginalized. A relationship between two men was even possible. Here I was also able to bring up what I felt to be a sin in confession. I did that a lot—at least whenever I'd been with another man. I even dated a man for several years, and I even felt like that was sinful. I had accepted the ecclesiastical commandments and rules as given. That's why I was never angry with the Church—because it was my fault.

When my boyfriend at the time suddenly died, I was very lonely. I felt alone in my shame. All I had left was my faith and job. It was then, for the first time in my life, that I prayed that God would send me a dear friend: someone with whom I could live and be happy.

Shortly thereafter, I met and fell in love with my current husband. It really was like a miracle. He's just as Catholic and religious as I am, but he didn't think our love was sinful. We went to our pastor and had a conversation. In doing so, I learned for the first time that love between two people, regardless of gender, is by no means punished by God with eternal damnation. We have since spoken often to clergymen about it, and it has been a completely new experience for me—to deal so actively and critically with the Catholic Church and its attitude toward homosexuality. I was finally able to stand tall and stand up for myself.

Good News for My People

Matthias Katsch
(born in 1963, publicist)

I like to sing. Always have. Even hymns like "A House Full of Glory Looks," "I Will Stand Firm to My Baptismal Promises," or "Great God, We Praise You."[1] Later, music helped me to survive and to embrace my feelings instead of becoming hardened.

As a child, I loved going to church on Sundays with my mother and then to special youth services held by the director of the student and youth ministry, my confessor.

Decades later, I understood that we were abused because we were Catholic. Because that's the reason why an overweight man with a slightly red face was allowed to ask me questions like if I ever masturbated, and if so, how often and how did I do it, and what fantasies I had when I did it. Questions that no adult would otherwise be allowed to ask a thirteen-year-old. It wasn't surprising, though, when it was a Catholic priest hearing confession.

---

1. *Ein Haus voll Glorie schauert, Fest soll mein Taufbund immer stehn,* and *Großer Gott, wir loben dich.*

Queerness IN THE Catholic Church

As a child, I was puzzled by the sentence: "I am not worthy that you should enter under my roof." Why was my mother always so affected by it? Why did she seem to feel "not worthy"? I found out only much later that it had something to do with her guilty conscience because I was born out of wedlock.

From then on, I felt unworthy too. There was something wrong with me when two priests abused my trust and assaulted me. After that, the realization slowly dawned upon my young self: you are gay.

As a young volunteer after graduating from high school, I was fascinated by the worship services of the Christian community in the slums of Santiago, Chile, where I worked with a project for children at risk: worship services without an organ but with a guitar and songs that came from the *Canto Nuevo* tradition, *Buenas nuevas pa' mi pueblo* ("Good news for my people").

At the same time, I met priests there who pursued me and unabashedly chatted me up. Significantly older than me, they tried to persuade me: "Look, it's not so bad, we have our fun too, but we don't talk about it. Become one of us." Here was the principle of Catholic double standards, perhaps a way of coping with one's own shame. At that moment, the offer seemed tempting: to become a respected, great priest like those who had abused me, to do something meaningful in life, instead of having quick sex in the public toilet at the train station. A great idea. The perfect temptation.

Thank God it didn't last long. At the first opportunity, I blurted out everything. It was my last confession. Today, I'm proud that I had the courage to stop lying and to accept that I couldn't belong. It took another two decades, however, before I had the courage to speak out.

After returning to Germany, I stopped attending church services and even avoided entering churches. If I ever do, it's because I'm visiting the great cathedrals of the West today because of their historical artwork.

What remained were the feelings—shame and anger above all. The shame emotionally chains me to the Church where I was abused, and it can still make me angry.

For over ten years, I have asked this Church to take responsibility for what it has done—through its priests and its teaching—in the lives of so many children and young people.

Standing Up for LGBTQIA+ People in the Church

Dr. Julia Knop
(born in 1977, professor of dogmatic theology)

For me, there are three important relationships to the subject of LGBTQIA+ people: first, as a person; second, as a Catholic; and third, as a professor of theology.

In their own way, relatives and friend circles reflect the diversity of lifestyles and relationships, and sexual identities and orientations. How could it be otherwise? Even among the older generation, I perceive a normalization in dealing with LGBTQIA+ people in private relationships. But I can still remember my family's "deafening silence" regarding the homosexuality of a relative who is now very old.

Such active silence is still commonplace in Church relations today. The Catholic Church simply fails in normalizing the subject of LGBTQIA+ people. The institutional contempt for male homosexuality particularly is too great—women slip through the cracks here—with a simultaneous high presence of LGBTQIA+ people among church employees. Too many are broken inside because they are denying an essential

Standing Up for LGBTQIA+ People in the Church

dimension of themselves or are hiding their romantic relationship to avoid jeopardizing their professional stability. Some become cold or cynical about it. Too many remain vulnerable to blackmail throughout their (professional) life. The exceptional conformity of clerics to the system does not always have religious reasons.

In theology, dealing with LGBTQIA+ subjects was taboo for a long time and in some cases still is. The reasons are well known. In the meantime, the willingness to be out publicly is growing. This is promoted by pastoral developments (marriage, family, and life counseling) and liturgical developments (blessing celebrations) that no longer take place under the institutional radar but are promoted and reflected by academies and (some) diocesan curiae. What is practiced (at length) and considered right and necessary should also be visible. There are—and need to be—good reasons for this. Good, constructive cooperation is developing here.

From my own experience, anyone who comes out in public becomes approachable, for better or for worse. People seek out contact on their own with any press release, a podcast, a public lecture on the (necessary) dogmatic reassessment of LGBTQIA+ subjects, or the argumentative support of couple blessings. There's "instruction," hate mail, and denunciation from the particularly devout. But there are also very beautiful, touching connections to LGBTQIA+ people who tell their story: classmates, college students, (former) priests, and priestly candidates from long ago who were previously unknown. Their stories demonstrate the destructive force that some ecclesiastical concepts, customs, and structures still wield. For example, it is frightening to hear the self-loathing regarding ideas about cultic purity or sinful sexuality that were thought to have long been overcome and can still trigger sensitive, spiritually gifted young people. Such ideas are not taught at the university, but they obviously live on in some religious milieus and perhaps in Church training contexts too. But there are also encouraging stories that tell of spiritual liberation and inner emancipation. Many, if not all, have (re)discovered a happy vitality and their place in life—sometimes also in the Church.

Their stories and their trust in telling them carry an obligation: good theology must reach this human *niveau* if it wants to speak credibly about God, who loves and bestows blessings on every creature as he created them.

Love Is the Visible Blessing of God in the World

Lisa Kötter
(born in 1960, freelance artist)

When I was young, I didn't know the terms "heterosexual," "homosexual," "gay," "lesbian," or "trans." A couple of women or men kissing on the street would certainly have unsettled me back then, since this image did not appear in my life, in my Catholic world. But it would not have caused any indignation in me.

Because, even then, I believed that we are known intimately by Divine Love. Divine Love who didn't create us to see us suffer, who doesn't rejoice at our suffering, who gave us life and desires, and who rejoices when we unwrap these gifts.

When I was young, it was hardly possible to talk about homosexuality. Whether at school or in the family, red warning lights of embarrassment flashed everywhere. Even to bring up this subject was to talk about things of the devil and sin. Even among friends, we first had to look for particular words and language to talk about sexuality in general and in its varieties. I remember how often we spoke with vulgarity to overcome our shame. Inwardly, however, we were very unhappy

Queerness IN THE Catholic Church

that we didn't have the appropriate language at our disposal to be able to have a good conversation with one another.

The discrepancy between what I specifically would call "good news" and the often condemning, merciless teaching of the Catholic Church has been a challenge for me that has accompanied me to this day. Mary 2.0[1] arose in part from these contradictions. Religions in general, and the Catholic Church in particular, have a strangely close relationship with sexuality.

Of course, it's about control. Because whoever controls such an elementary drive of life as sexuality has power over people down to their most intimate actions. Blaming people for their natural desires generates fear. And fear is the friend of the powerful.

Anyone who teaches sexuality and purity as opposites, who teaches sexuality itself to be unclean and only allowed, if at all, in a supposedly divinely ordained marriage, has a good chance of stirring up hatred in people's hearts. Hatred against those who do not correspond to this supposedly "divine order" and dare to live according to their nature.

The self-hatred that develops in people who have been subjected to this brainwashing and who discover sexual needs that do not correspond to this "order" can be very useful to a (religious) power apparatus. Sexuality is thus banished to the secret, dark backrooms of life. You create a moral problem of conscience and at the same time act as a savior in distress.

It's good that more people are coming out and realizing that they are loved and blessed as they are. And that the public no longer reacts (only) with hate and insults but also protects. It will be a long time before the pressure of religious delusions on queer people stops. The Churches are responsible, here, as the creators of this delusion.

---

1. See "Catholic Means Universal and That Includes Everyone," note 1.

Love Is the Visible Blessing of God in the World

Today I have (Catholic) relatives, friends, and acquaintances who come in every color of the rainbow. I am happy about the loving couple of grandfathers who look after their grandchildren so reliably. I comfort the friend who is stressed with her wife. I'm laughing my head off with a friend about the "awful" color choice of his nail polish. And I see more and more priests and ministers saying publicly, "Yes, your love is blessed. Because love is the visible blessing of God in the world."

I Want to Become a Priest, But...

Anonymous
(born in 1985, registered nurse)

From my early childhood and youth, I was fascinated by the beautiful worship services that we celebrated in the church all year round. Accordingly, I first served as an altar boy and later as a lector in my home parish.

At the age of fourteen, I realized that I felt attracted to the same sex, that is, the male gender. At the age of sixteen, I had my first homosexual experience. At about the same time, I started to desire devoutly to become a priest. And so, I entered a so-called minor seminary where I graduated from high school. During high school, I had a steady relationship with a fellow seminarian who was two years older than me, secretly, of course.

We were not the only male couple among the seminarians. We maintained a *Stammtisch*[1] and communicated in a secret language. It was clear to us that we could not expect

---

1. Literally, "regulars' table." An informal group that meets around a round table (the *Tisch*) often for casual conversation or deeper philosophical or political discussions.

I Want to Become a Priest, But...

any understanding from the seminary leaders for our homosexual disposition, of course. Similarly, if a seminarian had a relationship with a woman, this was not welcomed either, but it was at least tolerated. It was always said apologetically that this was part of the discernment and formation process to live celibately one day. I still do not understand this difference, because love is love.

After that, I entered the seminary of my home diocese. At that point, I broke off my relationship with my partner at the time—incidentally, he is now a priest in another diocese in Austria—for I was too afraid that someone would catch wind of it. It was difficult for me to let go of my love just to acquiesce to the demands of the Church and those of my superiors. I would not do that today, especially since the Church soon dropped me.

Various incidents and allegations had occurred in and around our seminary, creating strong media interest and prompting the Vatican to send Bishop Klaus Küng, an Opus Dei member, as an apostolic visitor.[2] I still remember a conversation with the visitor, whereby he insistently tried to get me to parrot his point of view. When I refused the "confession" he demanded of me—something that I felt was dishonest and forced on me—he summarily dismissed me from the seminary. The conversation was over in a second.

---

2. In July 2004, Bishop Klaus Küng was sent to the diocese of Sankt Pölten in Austria to investigate accusations of child pornography and homosexual relationships among the seminarians. There were apparently photos of seminarians fondling each other as well as charges of seminarians hoarding child pornography. One former student was arrested and sentenced to a six-month prison sentence for possession of child pornography, the bishop of the diocese resigned (and was replaced by Klaus Küng), and the seminary was closed. See, e.g., David Willey, "Pope Replaces Sex Scandal Bishop," *BBC News*, October 7, 2004, http://news.bbc.co.uk/1/hi/world/europe/3723638.stm.

Queerness IN THE Catholic Church

After that I was completely devastated, insecure, and afraid. I felt alone and without prospects. At the time, almost no one in the Church paid any attention to me; no one asked how I was doing, and no one was interested in how things were going with me. It seemed that this Church didn't care. I have not lost my faith and my trust in God. But my trust in the Catholic Church and its leaders—that's gone for good.

I Believed That I Wasn't Allowed to Be Gay

Christoph Krenzel
(born in 1993, 2D/3D artist for AR/VR applications)

In 2014, I fell in love with a man for the very first time in my life. I remember it like it was yesterday because, at the time, this was the most confusing and difficult moment of my life. The one thing I struggled with was admitting to myself that I had developed feelings for a person of the same sex: something I had feared might happen but had successfully repressed until then.

Until that point, being gay was simply unimaginable for me. On the one hand, this was because homosexuality simply did not exist in the environment in which I grew up, or it was kept secret. On the other hand, my conservative upbringing allowed only the classic image of love, marriage, and family to emerge in my head, which the Catholic Church still presents.

The topic of homosexuality was so alien to me for a long time. When I was called a "faggot" for the first time in the sixth grade, I first had to Google the term. To this day, I can still remember very clearly the ambivalent feelings that the search result aroused in me: on the one hand, there was excited curiosity; on the other hand, there was abysmal shame. From then on, I waged an inner struggle between my sexual orientation and my conception of how I had to be.

The main reason I couldn't be gay was because I wasn't as feminine as homosexuals were often portrayed. Yet somehow, I was different from my male classmates. Repeatedly, I was called "faggot," "homo," and so on—words that hurt me so much that I often restrained myself and acted very differently than I would naturally, just to avoid confirming this prejudice against myself. The inner struggle was taken to the extreme in 2014. Despite all my efforts, I had to admit that I had fallen in love with a man. Suddenly, at a party, I got to the point where I couldn't do it anymore. I burst into tears and in the middle of the night called my best friend—the only person in whom I felt I could confide with my dark secrets.

Following that moment, an incredibly difficult time began for me—a time in which I had to wrestle with myself, with my values, and with my faith, to accept what should never have happened. While I had to learn to accept myself anew every day, the fear of being rejected by others grew at the same time. I hid my first boyfriend from my family for over nine months. The fact that my younger brother had declared himself gay to my parents two years earlier didn't help at all. On the contrary, I thought a second gay man was asking too much from my family. I felt like I was punishing them. And they hadn't done anything wrong.

In the end, only my older brother had problems with my coming out. "You're not the brother I imagined anymore," he said. We didn't speak to each other for two years. In a rather unwilling encounter, I made it clear to him that he would have to decide whether we would remain a family or not. Against all expectations, he started to weep and clasped me in his arms.

I Believed That I Wasn't Allowed to Be Gay

Today we have discovered a closer connection to each other again, even if I still have to fight to be accepted for who I happen to be. But that's a process—a process that I haven't completed myself yet.

Two Gay Boys in Our Family

Ulrike Krenzel
(born in 1966, family coach and German teacher for refugees)

We're something of a Catholic "model family." I met my husband at *Katholikentag* in Munich.[1] Over time, we had four children, three boys and one girl, whom we took to church just as naturally as we had gone ourselves in our childhood. We also prayed together at home, talked about God, and tried to make our house open to everyone.

I never met a homosexual person in this Catholic "idyll" and therefore saw no need to concern myself with this topic. It just didn't come up in my life. And when it was briefly discussed, the traditional Church responses were quickly supplied.

And then one day, my youngest son came up to me. He was just fifteen years old. He said he needed to talk to me urgently and wept inconsolably. If he couldn't talk to me, he'd kill himself because he doesn't know what to do anymore. I was horrified. What can the problem be? He opened up only after I had repeatedly assured him that he could talk to me about anything. Finally, he said, "I'm gay."

---

1. See "A Gay Couple in the Church for Five Decades," note 3. *Katholikentag* was held in Munich in 1984.

Two Gay Boys in Our Family

So now it was out there. My thoughts were like a roller coaster in my head. What should I say now? My son waited for an answer, for a gesture. I took him in my arms and almost squeezed him, as a mother with her suffering child. He was my son; he was still the same. I told him I love him and there is no problem for me. He was relieved.

But I needed time to process this, and I told him so. He too had needed time to recognize and accept his sexuality. A period of deep reflection started for me. The thought that was most important to me: "Every human being is equally valuable, since every human being is created by God in God's own image."

The Church's statements regarding homosexuality now seemed like a farce. I was secretly hoping that my son was just going through a phase that would eventually go away. Today, of course, I know that's not the case, but it was part of my development and growth with the topic.

A good two years later, my oldest son approached me. He was twenty-two years old at the time. "Mom, I need to talk to you!" he said, pulling me into his room and crying. "Mom, you didn't do anything wrong; it's not your fault. I fell in love. It's a man."

The situation was like that of my youngest son. We cried, we talked, we hugged. He brought his boyfriend to our house for Christmas. He is a nice, open, young man who immediately won all our hearts.

But this time too I needed time to process the situation. In our family of all families—two gay boys. Although we considered ourselves open, it wasn't easy for us. Still, we talked and learned from each other.

The fact that the two boys were rejected by the Church when they came out was one of the most difficult things for all of us. They are both Catholic and their faith means a lot to them. It was the center of their life. They lost many of their friends and were not invited to their weddings.

The blessing service on May 9, 2021, was the beginning of a reconciliation between the Church and my older son. It was a step toward him—for whom faith is still just as important, but who felt rejected because he loves someone with all his heart and wants to share his life with him in good times and in bad.

Homosexuality as a Weapon

Ulrich Küchl
(born in 1943, priest and composer)

The commandment to love one's neighbor, although firmly connected with the commandment to love God, is usually interpreted in Church circles to suit the needs at the time. This is certainly the case when the topic of homosexuality is used as a weapon in connection with controversies among Church officials. I experienced this myself in 2004, when it came to the continuation or forced resignation of the then bishop of Sankt Pölten, Kurt Krenn. After all previous efforts had failed, as a last and unfortunately successful attempt, seminary employees of the Sankt Pölten seminary, including myself, were publicly accused of homosexuality.

Whether this claim was substantiated or not remained to be seen. In any case, it was a terrible experience of how homosexual people are despised and marginalized in the Catholic Church—and this happens even with the backing of the magisterium regarding sexual morality. I had to live through the trauma of many homosexual people being robbed of their human dignity and forsaken by the Church. This showed me existentially how fickle charity is in praxis.

Queerness IN THE Catholic Church

Bishop Klaus Küng, Dr. med., Dr. theol., the apostolic visitor entrusted with clarifying the alleged abuses in the Sankt Pölten seminary, made ample use of this sexual morality and of homophobic, right-wing, and minority opinions from the psychiatric world. Among other things, he suspected that people with homosexual desires had psychological anomalies, including their sexual desires. Indulging these was threatened with criminal consequences.

I was speechless to learn that the apostolic visitor had accused me of such anomalies. I therefore refused to accept the hiatus at a psychiatric facility he had requested, which he downplayed as a "conference center with specialist accompaniment."

He had my office inspected and searched my computer at work without my knowledge. Eventually, I was even forced to undergo a psychological and psychiatric evaluation in a forensic psychiatric institute! Of course, I was still not expecting myself to be portrayed as an alleged sex offender.

The apostolic visitor then used the entire arsenal of administrative discrimination, canon law sanctions, and media-facing gestures of power at his disposal to make it impossible for me to live openly and to persuade Bishop Krenn to resign. He eventually became his successor, all with the help of the "suspicions" of homosexuality! The apostolic visitor himself admitted to me several times that he had no evidence at all for his "suspicion." I wrote a book about my ordeal; it is titled *In Exile in Harmannsdorf: Memories of a Scandal*.[1]

Since then, I have at least been made "richer" by this painful experience. But this suffering is not over—at least not while the magisterium continues with its current position on

---

1. Fr. Küchl was the provost of the Eisgarn Abbey, renowned for its choirs and music, until Bishop Küng abolished it in 2009. Fr. Küchl went into a self-imposed exile to the village of Harmannsdorf, eighty miles (129 km) away from Eisgarn.

Homosexuality as a Weapon

homosexuality, which cannot be justified either theologically or in terms of charity. I am firmly convinced that it must and will be changed. Nevertheless, and precisely because of this, I repeat at this point what I wrote in the foreword of my book: "I am still a dedicated priest and deeply grateful to God."

We All Need Tolerance

Anonymous
(born in 1968, playwright and musician)

The fact that I can't reveal my name here makes me sad. I'm an established and openly gay man. I recognized my inclination early on and accepted it. I have been in a relationship with my partner for almost twenty-five years, and we've been married since 2015. I have enormous support from my family and circle of friends, and I have never experienced marginalization in my various professions.

And yet I now have reservations about making myself known here by name. The fear of being rudely contacted runs deeper than I wanted to believe. Too bad. Is it because I can't see the reader or meet her or him directly?

I have had good experiences with my confession that I am attracted to men. Unlike many others. Lucky. However, I never wanted to give my love life more forum than it deserves. I'm gay. Yes, of course. You can also point that out to me quietly. But first, I am me. Get to know me. And if it comes up in personal dealings—forgive me for the expression here—there's no way in hell I'll keep quiet about my gayness.

We All Need Tolerance

How many people sometimes hide that they believe in God? Maybe we need another outing soon: "Catholic? So what?!" I am in.

In my carefree childhood, there was a religious sister who had a strong influence on me. She encouraged me early on to follow my artistic path. And there were other people in the Church who influenced me positively. From the priest, whose catechism classes and sermons were so delightfully lively, to the pastor who leads the parish where I live today. When he quite unpretentiously blessed the rings for my husband and me, he gave us a blessing too, "Now you can actually give something to the notary. Now you already belong together."

Yes, I am Christian. I confess that I'm Catholic, even if it always surprises people. Even apart from the positive experiences that I had, I am firmly convinced that our society, our unity, would be so much poorer, and would collapse in some areas, if the Church, with all its people and support, did not exist. Retreat is not an option. Staying in it and enriching the community is better.

I simply believe in God. He is not a Christian, Jew, or Muslim. He is God—pure, all-encompassing, and above denominations.

And I believe that the Catholic Church today is good at its core, even despite a difficult history and many mistakes, beginning with the issue of homosexuality. Perhaps it would be time to introduce the word *homoamority*—Latins may forgive me this invention of the word—because it's not just about the sexual act. In the most blessed examples, it's about love; not wanting to be without the other. First, butterflies in the stomach… and in the heart. Then, a deep connection in the soul.

Finally, an analogy that the sister I mentioned earlier gave me a few years ago, "I decided to spend my life in the monastery. A life against the norm. I had to explain myself again and again. We both depend on tolerance. I can't really understand your life plan. Nor do I have to. But I can accept it, meet it with understanding. Your path doesn't have to be mine, just like mine wouldn't be yours. We just have to accept each other." Amen.

The Church's Sexual Morality and Its Victims

Michael Kurz
(born in 1964, retired)

I spent a large part of my childhood (1966–1976) in a children's home in Oberammergau. This home was funded by the city of Munich. When I lived there, it was run by Catholic religious sisters with good connections to a pastor from Cologne who regularly spent his "sex vacation" there. My time in children's homes was characterized by extreme psychological violence, extreme physical violence, and very serious sexual assaults.

This denied me any chance of believing in anything good from an early age to this day. How could one believe in a benevolent God whose "representatives" on earth have committed such terrible deeds on us children?

I've been homosexual for as long as I can remember, as I always say. I've never had a problem with it myself. From an early age, I was interested in science, and I soon found all Churches and matters of faith to be unrealistic. That's why I left the Catholic Church when I became self-reliant and independent. Since then, places of worship and all church establishments and events have been symbols of pure hypocrisy for me. I've avoided them for a long time.

Queerness IN THE Catholic Church

Over the years, however, I realized that I could neither forget nor repress what I had experienced in my childhood. It was still there. I ended up getting very sick, and after two suicide attempts, I had to undergo a long inpatient psychological treatment. How else could I have dealt with the topic? On my own initiative, together with a good therapist, I developed an "understanding of the perpetrator" that should not be confused with an understanding of the deed. I am convinced that there is always a reason or a cause for a person's actions.

And thus, I began to think of the perpetrators, the sisters and the priest. I noticed that this way of dealing with what I had experienced was good for me. That's how the topic of forgiveness suddenly came up for me. I don't know where this phrase came from, but I think it's true: "Forgiveness doesn't change the past, but it does enlarge the future."

From then on, yes, I began to reach out to the Church to reconcile with it. I soon discovered, however, that the Church doesn't want that at all; the Church just wants to cover it up. It wants to portray the victims of her completely dysfunctional sexual morality as either unbelievable or liars and, if it is cornered, foist ridiculous amounts of money and empty, insincere apologies on them.

During this time, I worked in the field of social care in various retirement homes and realized how important faith is for most people—and how important it is for the whole of society. Belief in God maintains a certain order. We humans cannot understand infinity, and we refuse to accept finiteness. Faith, however, helps most people come to terms with finitude.

I am even more stunned and angrier at what certain parts of the Church are doing at the moment. Clinging to their inhuman sexual morality is a slap in the face to believers and the many people who, in whatever way, work for or are involved

The Church's Sexual Morality and Its Victims

with them. In any case, I will continue to be a nuisance to the Church with my commitment to reconciliation. I express my sincere respect to all believers, but I tell them at the same time: Don't put up with what a few old men ask of you and do to you!

Before God, I Can Be Who I Am

Anonymous
(born in 1975, educator)

I only came to faith as a young adult and, after a long period of preparation, I was baptized in the Catholic Church. I didn't grow up with the Christian faith. It was my very personal decision to want to belong to God.

Later, I went to Erfurt to train as an educator at the Catholic technical school for educators,[1] connected to the Ursuline convent there. It was there that I fell in love for the first time with a woman, a classmate.

Around the same time, a friend invited me to her charismatic parish. From then on, I moved mainly in Free Church circles.[2] I had various experiences coming out in various churches. For example, in one I was thrown out of my small group; in another, I was no longer allowed to serve as a volunteer, and I even had to put up with an attempt by one group to pray for me to become "healthy."

---

1. *Katholischen Fachschule für Sozialpädagogik*, a training institute focused on practical skills—in this case for educators. This is meant to be advanced training for people who already have some initial training or experience.

2. Because the Evangelical Church in Germany (Lutheran) is the official state Church, other Protestant denominations are called "Free Churches."

Before God, I Can Be Who I Am

I even willingly underwent conversion therapy to be healed of my homosexuality. That was with the organization Desert Stream, which is called Living Waters in the United States. I did this because I felt so insecure about myself and because I was convinced that there was something wrong with me. Besides, I didn't want to continue to be thought of as a sinner.

That all does something to the soul. I became severely depressed, had to take medication, and had to go to the clinic many times. I also thought that God sees me as a sinner, even as sin incarnate. I felt like I wasn't allowed to be who I am. I was having a total identity crisis.

I really didn't want to have anything to do with God anymore then. But he kept sending me genuine Christians. And so, I gradually felt that God is not who people, especially those who are supposed to be very pious, think he is. Jesus died for me—that was how important it was to God that people are reconciled to him and that I am reconciled to him.

Project:Community,[3] where I have now worked for many years, helped me on the journey to self-acceptance. LGBTQIA+ Christians are welcome there to celebrate church services. Many of them there have experienced similar marginalization as I have.

It's been a long struggle to find my true self, to accept me, and to know and feel that God accepts me and loves me just as I am. Of course, I make mistakes and wrong decisions. But God loves me despite everything. He won't let go of me.

I can come to him, and before him I can be who I am: a woman who loves women. I have been with a wonderful woman for six years now. We've been married for two years.

---

[3]. *projekt:gemeinde* is an evangelical-style Baptist Church in Vienna with an emphasis on social justice. Their website is projekt-gemeinde.at.

I Am Grateful to the Church— And Struggle with It

Michael Langer
(born in 1978, chemist and organist)

I realized from a young age that I was attracted to boys but never spoke openly about it for the first nineteen years of my life. In part, this was because the topic of sexuality was generally taboo in my parents' house and, in part, because I allowed myself to be intimidated by the rather conservative values and negative attitude of the people in my immediate environment toward homosexuals.

I was enthusiastic about the Church as a child and felt a close connection to it. At the age of seven, I was allowed to serve as an altar boy. I also became a lector at an early age. The term *church* for me at that time referred mainly to the local church, the parish to which I belonged. It was a very active parish in which I became more and more involved over the years, mainly in music.

It also gave me stability and support due to my difficult living conditions. Some of the people there became role models

I Am Grateful to the Church—And Struggle with It

who helped me orient my life. As a result, my home parish became like a big family and played a central role in my life until adulthood. I thought it was beautiful to belong, to pray together, to sing, to make music, to work, and, of course, to celebrate together.

But during this time, I struggled more and more with my feelings for people of my own sex, for the reasons mentioned above. An unwanted outing at the age of nineteen became a hard caesura, but it also set off a positive process in me. Over time, I have learned to stand by my homosexuality.

I wanted to study theology and become a priest, so I graduated from a religious college after high school. But I soon realized that this shouldn't be my path because it had become much more important to me to stand by myself and not to deny my homosexuality, which is an essential part of who I am.

In this context, I got to know people in the Church, including clergy, who, on the one hand, vehemently rejected homosexuality, if not even demonized it, but on the other, were homosexual themselves and lived a secret homosexual life. For example, I met a man through a gay dating app who I later found out was a priest. He was imagining having a secret relationship with me. For me, then as now, a relationship based on a game of hide-and-seek was and is out of the question.

Despite all the ambivalence, I remain loyal to the Church, even if I don't understand why unconditional love between two people of the same sex should be worth less than love between a man and a woman. Despite all the negative experiences regarding how homosexuality is handled within the Church, I live my faith. For example, I have been a part-time organist for many years.

Queerness IN THE Catholic Church

But there is another reason why, despite everything, I have not yet turned away from the Catholic Church. The Church, specifically my home parish, gave me support during an extremely difficult time in my life. It was there for me like a family when all I needed was a stable living environment. I am grateful for that to this day.

I Want You to Be Happy

Patrick Lindner
(born in 1960, *schlager*[1] singer)

My husband and I got married in autumn 2020. It was even more important to us to receive God's blessing in the Church after the civil wedding. Contrary to expectations, we were able do this without any problems—in a Catholic church, by a Catholic priest. Why was that important to us? Quite simply, for us, when two people say, "I do," to each other, the blessing of God is simply part of it. Without a blessing, we would have been missing something. Our wedding guests and we were amazed by the celebration but also by the fact that the Catholic Church is obviously able to do more than the Vatican thinks it can.

    I grew up in a Catholic environment but was not brought up strictly Catholic. When we were visiting our relatives in the country during my childhood, going to church on Sundays

---

    1. *Schlager* is a German music genre, characterized by sentimental lyrics and catchy melodies. It often appeals to an older audience who enjoy the traditional German idiom, yet there are examples of contemporary pop/schlager crossovers that are nearer to modern American pop songs. Patrick Lindner is well-known for his singing and acting, for being openly gay, and for adopting a Russian child with his husband at the time. He remains a popular entertainer in Germany.

was always a must. That bothered me back then. It wasn't going to church itself that bothered me, but the obligation to go. When faith becomes a must, something essential is lost, namely, freedom. I believe that God calls people to freedom and rejoices when people live in freedom.

This also applies to sexuality. In my childhood and adolescence, sexuality was not an issue that was discussed—and certainly not homosexuality. It wasn't until I went to a technical school for hospitality management that I met people who helped me, at least to come out to my family. Until then, I had had to navigate my sexuality completely on my own. After I came out to my family, I was schlepped to a doctor. He treated me as if I were sick and warned me of the difficulties I was about to face. I should think this through carefully, he said.

For a long time, I thought I had to play the role that the public expected of me. When I hopefully considered coming out, I was advised not to. I was warned that if I did, my entire career would be at stake. In 1999, I did it anyway. Indeed, I did have to restart a little bit from the beginning. While most of my fans still stood by me and supported me, some turned on me. A few even wrote me angry letters. They almost all came back, however, when they realized that I was still the same as before.

Since then, it has been very important for me to support young people in the phase of growing up and finding themselves. It is important to help them find an accepting and appreciative environment in this important phase of life. Young people, in particular, should be able to discover and accept their gender identity and sexual orientation without prejudice and pressure. They should be able to live with confidence. To this end, I founded the Patrick Lindner Foundation in 2013, which promotes equality for lesbian, gay, and other queer people and works to reduce discrimination, marginalization, and violence.

I Want You to Be Happy

One of my songs says: "Once I wanted to feel what it's like when you kiss from a free heart and don't miss anything anymore. Once I wanted to love without fear of what another might say just because you're dancing to a different tune. I built up the courage, then I told her: 'Mom, I feel different.' And she just said, 'I want you to be happy—every day! You only live once, not twice or three times. I want you to be happy!'"[2] I wish Mother Church had the same attitude!

---

2. Patrick Lindner, *Ich will, dass du Glücklich bist. Ich feier die Zeit: Das Beste zum Jubiläum* (Telamo, 2020).

The Brother's*[1] Distress

Gudrun Lux
(born in 1980, city councilwoman)

When I recently campaigned for the recognition of queer people and lifestyles in a debate, someone asked me, "Why are you going out on a limb again? You're not affected at all." I was born and raised a girl, I live as a woman, I am married to a man, and we have two children. In short, we're the cookie-cutter family. I'm still affected. I'm affected when my brothers* and sisters* are wronged. I am affected when people who do not fit into simple categories are marginalized and humiliated. Theologically, we are all members of one body; if one part is wronged, it must not and cannot leave the other indifferent.

In my everyday life—I've been active in Alliance 90/The Greens[2] since I was a teenager, today as a city councilor

---

1. The *genderstern*, "gender star," represents the many endings that personal nouns may take in German grammar to express the range of gender expressions those words refer to. For example, *Katholikin* refers to one Catholic woman, *Katholik* to one Catholic man, *Katholikinnen* to multiple Catholic women, and *Katholiken* to multiple Catholic men (which traditionally referred to a mixed group as well). The gender star, usually placed after the root word and before the noun endings (*Katholik*innen*), is a linguistic sign of gender inclusion. It is used frequently throughout this book in the German but is usually untranslated as English is a far less gendered language.

2. See "A Gay Couple in the Church for Five Decades," note 2.

The Brother's* Distress

of the state capital, Munich—sensitivity to gender roles is relevant, overcoming clichés, and the freedom of people to find themselves, without having to fit in to such simple categories. But I've also been Catholic since I was a child; it's part of my identity to take on responsibility in the Church, to help shape it.

What was long unthinkable in the Catholic Church can now be said and discussed: the spectrum of gender diversity, the spectrum of sexual desire. Yes, there are intersex and trans, nonbinary, homosexual, asexual, and bisexual people. Yes, even in the Church. And yes, like all other people, they deserve full respect and recognition for their way of life, their life in its entirety. We no longer tolerate as taboo the fact that gender identity and sexuality can and may change over the course of a lifetime, that different facets of people can come forward—or step back—in different phases of life. For many, this is alien; for some it is frightening if it shakes, disturbs, and destroys their own worldview.

Just a few years ago, even speaking of homosexuality in the Church was a scandal (often not homosexuality itself, mind you). Today, youth synods who speak freely about their gender identity are taking part in the Synodal Path—and they are being listened to. One small step? Maybe. A step in the right direction anyway. In spring 2021, after a truly crucial vote, the Central Committee of German Catholics (*ZdK*),[3] to which I belong, was able to push through the "gender star" as part of our official spelling in internal and external communication. That was a happy day for me. With this, the highest committee of laity in Germany recognizes gender diversity,

---

3. The *Zentralkomitee der deutschen Katholiken* is a lay organization made up of representatives from other German Catholic organizations. Among other things, they are responsible for organizing the *Katholikentag*, mentioned in "A Gay Couple in the Church for Five Decades," note 3.

names it, and makes it visible. One small step? Maybe. But a sign that gives me courage.

We can change the world by what we do, even if it's only by small steps. I see it as my duty to demand respect and recognition for my queer brothers* and sisters*, but also to promote and offer safe spaces in which they can speak and exist freely. Be it at a synodal meeting, in the home parish, or in the Catholic organization. Because I am affected: "How does God's love abide in anyone who has the world's goods and sees a brother or sister in need and yet refuses help?" (1 John 3:17).

The Rainbow Is a Bridge between Heaven and Earth

Fady Maalouf
(born in 1979, singer and artist)

For a long time, I've wondered why I had to hide. Truth, while inviolable, has many faces depending on one's perspective.

The truth is always the same but somehow always different. Some see it clearly, and others see it warped. Some look at it up close, others at a distance. And often the truth becomes a twisted illusion.

At a certain point, the truth about myself was very clear to me because I was closest to it, and that is true of every creature in the universe, of every star, of every ray of light.

If you want to judge me, I invite you to come a few steps closer, maybe walk with me for a while; I will even give you my shoes for it. Open not only your eyes but also your heart; maybe then you can understand me.

I grew up in the Church and attended Mass with my mother every Sunday. Our small cozy apartment in my Lebanese homeland was always full of priests, religious chanting, rosary prayers, and the overwhelming scent of incense.

Queerness IN THE Catholic Church

These rituals made me feel very comfortable and safe, especially during the war times when I was born. When the bombs fell outside, I would sleep, hugging a statue of Mary; that's what made me feel safe. I still have that statue.

That all started to change when children and adults suddenly started turning away from me or swearing at me. I didn't understand why. I only knew that I would rather sing, paint, and dance than play football.

My best friends at school stopped talking to me because their parents told them to. They pushed me away or, worse, hit me. One even knocked out my tooth once. But it violently broke my heart too.

From that moment, I understood that the cruelest kind of loneliness is when you are still surrounded by people but ignored by them, as if you suddenly ceased to exist. I would become virtually invisible unless someone felt like taunting me.

A few years later, as I hit adolescence, I began to recognize for myself that I was different. Then, I embarked on a long journey of self-discovery filled with spiritual anguish, fears, and frustrations.

The pinnacle of this torment was when a priest preached about people like me. He said that we should all be burned and damned! It was the same priest who came to our house every week, ate next to me at our table, and told me what a great young man I was!

I remember suddenly standing there paralyzed. It felt like an arrow pierced my chest and tore it apart. I felt this cruel sermon to be the ultimate betrayal of Jesus's message. These hateful words triggered a deep sadness and anger within me—a state that lasted for years.

But the voice of Jesus is stronger than the clamor of this fallen world. And so, after a long time, I entered a chapel again,

The Rainbow Is a Bridge between Heaven and Earth

stood in front of the cross, and realized that I am a part of it: just like Jesus, I too was rejected, despised, and mistreated.

I cried and made peace with myself and with God. Love triumphs over ignorance, and ignorance is the sister of evil. Today I carry my light and my cross with pride. And for me, the rainbow is a bridge between heaven and earth!

God Is Love
Christof Gabriel Maetze
(born in 1965, bank clerk)

I was born into an enlightened diaspora Catholic family in West Berlin. Church and faith have been part of my life from the beginning: attending Sunday services, going to St. Engelbert Catholic Elementary School, being a member in the German Scout Association of St. George[1] from cub to leader, and, of course, after my first communion, becoming an altar boy. My father was a member of a Catholic fraternity with Jesuit roots. I had many long, good conversations with him about faith and about the trustee of faith on earth, the Church.

Later, we moved to a small town in Westphalia, where again, as Catholics, we were in the minority. Church, parish, and the scouts were my extended family. I felt woven into these things, which obviously were always important to me. Faith and Church really supported me, especially during the difficult times of adolescence and when I was separated from my family. I felt supported because I was always aware, "Lord,

---

1. The *Deutsche Pfadfinderschaft Sankt Georg* is the largest youth scouting organization in Germany. It is similar to the Girl Scouts and Boy Scouts of America, with an emphasis on developing well-rounded, respectful, caring, and engaged young citizens. The *DPSG* is open to boys and girls of all faiths, who begin as *wölflinge* ("cub scouts") and progress through the highest rank of *Rover* between the ages of sixteen and twenty. To be a leader, one must be over eighteen.

God Is Love

I am not worthy that you should enter under my roof, but only say the word and my soul shall be healed."

In my early twenties—now living in Frankfurt am Main—I came out. Instead of hiding like before, I was now open about my gayness: with my family, at work, and in the Church. Shortly thereafter, the pastor asked me to talk with him. He told me that my involvement in Catholic youth ministry and as a leader of holiday camps, even interacting with young people, was no longer appropriate. My orientation, he said, was not sinful, in itself, but consummated homosexual acts constituted a mortal sin. If I wished to continue to belong to my extended family of the Church, it would require that I completely abstain from same-sex sexuality. For me, that was out of the question. So that I would not be at a loss for words, I looked for suitable quotes from the Bible and countered him. At the end of the discussion, however, I decided to resign from the Church rather than be thrown out.

And so, my time as a beloved leader in Catholic youth ministry came to an end along with being expelled from the larger community of God because his representatives on earth took offense at my sexual orientation. It took me a long time to really understand that, and it didn't feel good. It felt like the ground was suddenly pulled out from under my feet. After a long and painful process of finding out who I really was, I was expelled from the Catholic family just because, as a man, I love and desire men. This made me angry and lonely. I was out.

My relationship with the Church hasn't been the same since. It has become more distant. Over the years, I have maintained my faith, but as something very personal. The trustees of faith with their supposed monopoly on truth are barely in contact with me anymore. What keeps me going are phrases like this, "God is love, and those who abide in love abide in God, and God abides in them" (1 John 4:16).

Agape and *Eros* — Two Sides of the Same Coin

Anonymous
(born in 1950, journalist)

I was thirteen or fourteen years old, a student at a Catholic classical-language high school in a medium-sized German university town, an acolyte, then senior acolyte, a lector, and a member of a Catholic youth group.

The term *gay* existed, but it wasn't part of my active vocabulary. I knew the word *homosexual*, but it took me a while to apply it to myself. I already knew, though, that men interested me more than women and girls. And I also had — precocious as I was — sexual contact with young men, not just with classmates or boys of the same age.

And then we had a spiritual retreat in our school led by a Jesuit priest. Through a "shortened" Jesuit retreat, he wanted to bring Christianity and the teachings of the Catholic Church closer to us young students and also bring them closer to redemption, eternal life, Jesus, Mary, and the saints. A lot of things that are still important to me in my life today.

The priest not only wanted to teach us the great mysteries of salvation and the love of God, but also the sexual morality

Agape and *Eros*—Two Sides of the Same Coin

of the early 1960s: chastity, continence, self-discipline. It was awful; it was scary. Hell was waiting, not just purgatory.

That wasn't for me. So, when—toward the end of the week of reflection—it was time for confession, I did not confess a single transgression of the sixth commandment. It was clear to me that what I felt and what I did (already back then) was not a sin. Because the God who loves me and who guides my life made me the way I am. And that can't be a sin because it's his "handiwork."

Love, physical affection, even sex are gifts from God. That was and is my attitude. I have maintained this attitude throughout my life, even when I entered the seminary with the aim of becoming a Catholic priest. For over two years, I had an intimate relationship with another seminarian—physically, emotionally, intellectually, and spiritually.

We both believed in God who loves us, and in Jesus, the redeemer of our guilt and the companion of our lives. Even if we had spent the night together, we would go to Mass together, to holy communion together, to the love-feast. *Agape* and *eros*—two sides of the same coin!

My companion has since become a priest, and he has even risen to quite a high position in the Church hierarchy. I didn't become a priest; I became a journalist.

We both stayed Christians—Catholics even. We believe in love; in the love of God for people, and in the love of people for one another. We both hope for salvation and eternal life, and we are sure that we will see each other again there.

My Child Is Transgender — What's Wrong with That?

Iris Molsbeck
(born in 1968, elderly care assistant)

Since I was thirteen, I have always lived in a place that has been very Catholic, where everyone knows everyone and hardly anything remains hidden. Social life is very much determined by traditions, customs, and habits. Probably the most important principles for the community life of people there to this day are "It's always been like this" and "We've never done it that way!"

The Catholic faith has therefore always played a major role in my life. Even if I don't go to church every Sunday, I feel at home and safe in the Catholic Church. I didn't hear too much of the long-standing discussions about Catholic sexual morals. To be honest, I have to admit, I wasn't really interested in them.

My Child Is Transgender—What's Wrong with That?

I am the proud mother of two children. One of my kids eventually didn't want to wear girls' clothes, and eventually didn't want to be a girl at all anymore. One day it[1] said to me, "Mom, I'm transgender." At that point, I didn't even know what that meant. I had to swallow, but then I said to my child, "That's okay. You are fine the way you are." Afterward, I found out what it actually means when someone is transgender and what all that entails. But what the pope and the Vatican say about it didn't interest me then. It still doesn't really interest me, today.

At the beginning, I suspected the path would be difficult for my child as a transgender person.

It's not easy for me and my family either, but we stick together. Countless visits to doctors, psychologists, and lawyers were necessary before everything could take its course. During one of the first conversations, a psychologist said to my child, "You should be real happy that your family is standing behind you. Unfortunately, it is common for someone who comes out as transgender to be rejected by their family. Then they're absolutely alone."

I'm pretty sure there was a lot of talk about our family in town then. That's still the case now. I don't care. If people want to talk, let them talk. In any case, no one ever asked me about the fact that one of my children was transgender. Once, however, it so happened that I got into a conversation with our

---

1. *Eines Tages sagte es zu mir*... Literally, the pronoun is the nonpersonal "it." This is perhaps intentional, even if unusual. According to the Non-Binary Wiki (https://nonbinary.wiki/wiki/Pronouns#German_neutral_pronouns), some German nonbinary individuals choose *es* for their pronoun to "reclaim" it. It is unclear whether this author is using the pronoun this way or if she is using it incorrectly when another pronoun would be more appropriate.

Queerness IN THE Catholic Church

Catholic pastor about it. He just said, "Then that's the way it is. Your child will always be your child!" These words did me a lot of good.

The Catholic faith helped me to deal with my many questions and concerns. But for me, faith has nothing to do with a person's gender identity or sexual orientation. A person is what they are. And they are wanted by God, just the way they are. What's bad or wrong with that?

Praying It Away Doesn't Work

Anonymous
(born in 1970, priest and psychotherapist)

At the age of sixteen, I first walked into the seminary of my home diocese. It was a world of its own, a purely male world, to be precise with well over a hundred seminarians. The seminary had contact days to get to know others there.

I joined four years later as a young gay man. Being gay—I didn't even dare to say the word at the time. Could someone else be gay too? I gave no sign. I felt too afraid of "it," afraid that someone would notice.

Luckily, I found a few allies over the years. No, we didn't have sex with each other. That was a no go! But we did confide in each other.

The in-house administration shunned the subject almost like the devil shuns holy water. A group of us seminarians once had a conversation with one of the people responsible for our formation. It was about the question of whether a homosexual person could be recognized by appearance. I still remember his answer today; in a tone of conviction, he said, "Oh, gentlemen, I beg you, I can recognize whether someone is homosexual using common sense!"

Queerness IN THE Catholic Church

He didn't recognize us. We were all gay in the group. So were about 60 percent of all the seminarians, if not more. So much for knowledge of human nature. So much for clichés.

However, the spiritual director, who was so spiritual that at times he seemed almost disembodied, simply gave us the general advice of "bring *'it'* to the Lord!" Meaning, we should pray it away. But that didn't work. Neither the desire for being content with oneself nor the desire for physical closeness could simply be prayed away.

It was then that the first rumors started surfacing that homosexuals could not be ordained. The trembling began. Did they see through us? No. The conversation with the bishop before the consecration went well. "You're in a priestly community; that should help," he said regarding sexuality. In fact, he wasn't wrong about that. Nevertheless, it was difficult for me to talk about "it."

After ordination, I spent the first six years as a chaplain in various parishes. Then came my first job as pastor. No easy years. The way was difficult. I didn't make it and broke celibacy many times. I was able to come out as gay to friends, but not to everyone. Within the Catholic milieu it seemed inconceivable to me that one could accept "it," let alone like it. Didn't one immediately assume a nocturnal life in the scene? Wouldn't one even be considered a pedophile?

Looking back today, I see how important it was that we could at least talk openly in the ordination course and with some of my confreres. I've often asked myself, "Why didn't they try to address the fear that raged within us and knocked at the doors of the soul at night? Why is gay sexual identity still demonized in the Church?"

I know so many gay priests who carry out their work in a professional, creative, and philanthropic manner! So many who worship with liturgical sensitivity. So many who are more empathetic when talking to the suffering, sick, and dying than

Praying It Away Doesn't Work

others who compensate for their longings with alcohol, gambling, or secret visits to brothels.

Yes, the fear accompanied me too. But my faith in this man called Jesus finally overcame this fear. Certainly, I gave up my priesthood for this. Like so many others. I know one thing for sure: I couldn't pray "it" away and I don't want to pray "it" away either. I have found a wonderful partner to live with. I'm fine as a gay ex-priest. But I confess, sometimes I wonder how it could have been different.

Why I Am Not Catholic, Unlike My Wife

Almut Münster
(born in 1970, social worker and child/youth psychotherapist[1])

My wife, Christine, is Catholic and her faith is important to her. That's why we both let the #lovewins campaign bless us together. That blessing was very moving. Surprisingly, apart from the importance for our relationship, this service had no religious significance for me. Surprisingly, because there is usually too much that irritates me in the Catholic Church; because I can't find any connection between this Church and my life, my feelings, my faith.

    I'm reluctant to put God—or whatever you want to call "that"—in concrete terms, because I find this presumptuous given my little common sense. And I can't believe that the Church knows any better—since they only have common sense as well. My faith and my feelings don't fit well into the Catholic Church, but neither do they really fit into any other religion. As a result, I lack the appropriate forms to celebrate worship services, to be able to celebrate in community, to live

---

1. In German, these nouns are explicitly feminine.

Why I Am Not Catholic, Unlike My Wife

my faith, and to express it in a way that suits me, although religiosity and faith are very important to me. It's a real shame and I miss it. From my professional experience, I can say that I am not the only one missing it.

How beautiful was the openness at the blessing, to feel welcome, to be able to worship in community, to be blessed. Many years ago, in a church in a Brazilian favela, I found the Church to be similarly welcoming and open. I was deeply impressed by the social commitment of the people there, the faith they lived, the power conveyed by faith, and the community of faith, as well as the willingness to adopt innovative, social, and inclusive political positions. This church conveyed to the people that they are welcome with their respective needs, in their individual being, and in all their diversity.

I wish for the Church to become more compatible with our current reality of life and our modern level of knowledge, that it become more diverse and more open to individual forms of faith and life. Faith, prayer, rituals, and religious community are very important for us as humans. And an institution that credibly represents ethical—but humane—values in our market-oriented society, I think, is just as important. I wish it for myself, and I wish it for the Church.

Better to Resign from the Priesthood than to Lead a Double Life

Otto Johann Piplics
(born 1970, priest and singer)

My mother was always happy to tell me that when I was a small child I wanted to be pope. I was aware of the TV broadcasts of the *Urbi et Orbi* blessings from Rome from an early age. In elementary school, I wanted to be an altar server as early as possible. Then my career aspirations became more defined. Following the example of our pastor, whom I admired very much, I wanted to become a priest. Consequently, I went to the archbishop's boys' seminary until my high school graduation.[1]

    During that time, I prayed often to become a good priest. During puberty, I realized how erotically attractive boys and men were to me. But as a priest, I would be celibate and so it shouldn't matter. After graduating from high school, my path immediately led to the priestly seminary. Since music was

---

    1. *...bis zur Matura.* The *matura* is one of two commonly used secondary school finishing exams. It is more like A-Levels in the UK or the similar *abitur* in Germany than it is to America's SAT or ACT.

always very important to me, I also studied singing at the conservatory along with theology.

After my ordination, I started pastoral work with great joy. I can still remember the exhilaration I felt when I was assigned my first parish. It felt like how I thought a lover should feel! I was fully committed to my new role and trying to use my talents to build up the Church and the kingdom of God.

Being celibate was easy for me because I was busy with parish work, preparation and celebration of the sacraments, children and youth ministries, and, last but not least, the Passion Play, which was a tradition in my parish and dictated parish life every five years. I had already led three seasons and prepared the fourth. In addition, I had been elected dean, had been given a second parish, and was supposed to help with the diocesan renewal process.

Gradually, however, I fell into a state of exhaustion; my health problems included significant obesity, high blood pressure, and prediabetes. At the same time, the loneliness of celibacy that had always been particularly difficult for me turned into a burdensome loneliness. It was then that I said to a friend for the first time, "I'm gay!"

This was the turning point when I began to take more responsibility for myself again. I said no a lot, started exercising, and lost nearly ninety pounds. I clearly felt the longing for relationship and intimacy, and I allowed myself to feel these longings. That's what led to me kissing another man for the first time at the age of forty-seven. I also read much about homosexuality and the Church, and I began to think about it more theologically.

It soon became clear that, under these circumstances, I would not be able to carry out my ministry in the Church as before. How was I supposed to continue to advocate and represent an institution that calls homosexuality a "grave depravity"[2] and categorically obliges people to be chaste because of their sexual orientation? As part of this group of people and as a theologian, how could I avoid dealing with the fact that the justifications given by the Church do not stand up to either the test of human science or biblical exegesis? I therefore followed a word of Pope Francis: "It is better for them to resign the priesthood than for them to lead double lives."

I am hopeful that I will be shown where my path is leading me and where God might have a place for me and my vocation. I am now taking a university course in cultural management[3] and hope to get back on my feet professionally in this way. I run my small household and try to stay healthy, nourished, and fit. I've been baking my own bread for a year and a half, and I hope to break it and share it with someone I love.

---

2. CCC 2357.

3. *Kulturmanagement* refers to managing theaters, museums, and other such places of "culture."

Why I Do Not Need Any Church

Ansgar Pippel
(born in 1955, retired)

I come from a small town in Hochsauerland, where I was born the sixth of eight children. From the beginning, life was not easy for me. When I was only three months old, I became so ill that I almost died. As a result of this disease, my right eye was permanently misaligned. With my severely impaired eyesight, the other children thought I was clumsy and stupid. I was teased, beaten, and ostracized.

I also felt different from the other boys from an early age. I didn't want to play football with them and had different interests, and therefore, no friends. Instead, I preferred to be with girls. I felt comfortable when I was playing with them.

When I grew up, I was sent to a school in Paderborn for the blind and visually impaired. At first, I felt rejected, but I soon realized that my classmates had very similar or even greater problems than I did. That gave me a boost. My happiness was short-lived, however, because my visual impairment was not severe enough to allow me to stay at the school. I had to return to my hometown where the bullying continued.

Queerness in the Catholic Church

I tried to hide my difference as much as possible so as not to make my problems bigger. After school, I apprenticed as a restaurant manager. I met a woman who I married just a year later. After three years, our daughter was born, and after another five years, our son. Although everything seemed fine on the outside, our marriage eventually fell apart.

I finally had to admit to myself what I knew to be true: I liked men; I was gay. Still, I kept up the heterosexual façade. A relationship with a new female partner lasted twelve years. But at some point, I started dating men secretly. I had several affairs, none of which lasted long. That changed only when I met my current husband, by chance, at work. It was love at first sight.

With him, I experienced for the first time what I had sorely missed in the previous decades of my life: mutual desire and mutual intimacy, affection and solidarity, honesty and understanding—in short, real love. My happiness was made complete by the fact that my kids reacted well when I came out and they accepted my new partner.

I spent my childhood and youth in a strongly Catholic environment. The Catholic faith was pervasive; what the Church taught and what the pastor said was law. Everything was ordered according to Catholicism. But there was no place for me and my difference in this order. I did not find the protection and support in the Church that I so urgently needed at the time. I found the protection and support I need today elsewhere. And that's why I no longer need the Church.

I Am a Learner

Gregor Podschun
(born in 1990, national chairman of the
German Catholic Youth Federation, BDKJ[1])

I have been active in Catholic youth organizations since my childhood: through scouting,[2] in the Catholic rural youth organization,[3] in the Young Catholic Community,[4] and as chairman of the BDKJ at all levels. I grew up in a traditional Catholic family; my grandfather was a deacon and my parents were very involved in the Church. Serving as an acolyte and as a chorister was natural to me, as was working with confirmation candidates and serving in a youth center. My entire life has been shaped by my Catholicism. It shapes my life and is part of my identity.

For a long time, the question of people's gender identity was not an issue for me. I, myself, am a straight cis man and

---

1. The *Bund der Deutschen Katholischen Jugend* (BDKJ) is an umbrella organization with leaders and representatives from all the major Catholic youth organizations in Germany.

2. Likely referring to the *Deutsche Pfadfinderschaft Sankt George*; see "God Is Love," note 1.

3. Likely referring to the *Katholische Landjugendbewegung Deutschlands*, a Catholic youth organization for children and young people living in rural areas.

4. The *Katholische jugend Gemeinde*; see "Finding the Strength to Come Out," note 1.

Queerness IN THE Catholic Church

not affected by discrimination. At the same time, I was fine with giving everyone love and accepting the sexuality they claim for themselves. Then, when I started actively working at the BDKJ, my awareness of the problem of how the Catholic Church deals with LGBTQIA+ people increased. Around the same time, I began my studies in social work with a focus on gender justice and learned about the suffering of people.

The youth associations offer an opportunity to stand up for change in the Church. They allow people to get involved as supporters of LGBTQIA+ rights in society and in the Church. At the same time, I noticed how much harm I caused myself through my ignorance and my involvement in a heteronormative system. I got to know many people who revealed new perspectives for me. They showed me where my thinking, behavior, and words were either hurtful or too narrow and where I needed to improve.

Too often, I still think in old patterns and get trapped in my old worldview. I need people to open it up for me and I need to be willing to let myself be opened up. This is a Christian attitude—allowing for something new, interpreting the signs of the times, and thus increasing the freedom of others and one's own freedom at the same time.

And then there are the moments that make me despair—a Church in which suffering happens again and again, which denies the discrimination it exudes, in which human rights are posed as if they were up for discussion, and in which systematic violence is made possible. The Catholic Church especially values tradition and power over the ethical imperative of altruism and preventing violence.

Encountering people saves me from this—in the youth associations, with other allies, with those affected who, despite the injuries, are fighting for themselves, for others, and for

I Am a Learner

their Church as well. That gives me courage and strength to keep going. I need to keep learning, get better, share my worries and fears, spread courage and hope, and stand up so that our Church can become a place that is equally open to all people and thus proclaims the true gospel. I need to do this very concretely.

"But If I Do Not Have Love…"

Peter Priller
(born in 1961, priest and social worker)

When I was ordained a priest at the Freising Cathedral in 1991, I had long been aware of my sexual orientation as a gay man. It was also clear to me that the issue of celibacy affected me no differently than it did a heterosexual candidate for ordination. Yes, like most, I accepted the obligation to be celibate. I honestly thought I could make it work somehow, and if I ever failed at abstinence, it would be part of the "internal forum"[1] and would be something I could fix with a confessor or a spiritual director. That's what I thought, and that's how many candidates for ordination think, no matter whether they are attracted to men or women.

What I didn't expect was love, which, according to 1 John 4:7, comes from God. In fact, I hadn't even considered God, I must admit now. When I first became a chaplain in Bad Tölz, love came in the form of an extremely attractive mustache. I

---

1. A distinction made in canon law. An "internal forum" issue affects the individual and their relationship to God, rather than the "external forum," which deals with the social and corporate good.

"But If I Do Not Have Love…"

quickly found out who was behind it, and at the end of my first year, we met, Sepp and I, at his old house.

It was a long evening, and I warmly smoked my tobacco pipe several times. Walking back to the vicarage at three o'clock in the morning, I knew my life was about to change. Of course, you don't just throw your entire life plan overboard. Three years of secrecy followed. At some point, however, we both realized that a decision had to be made. I chose love and requested an appointment with my archbishop. Then things took their course….

But what was also clear to me at the time was that being a priest, being a pastor—at the grassroots level—was my calling. And as a theologian, I had reflected on the concept of Church to such an extent that it was clear to me that the Church as such "subsists" in the denominational Churches but that no denominational Church is the Church of Jesus Christ— not even the Catholic Church. I remembered that, even as a student at the end of a Church history class, I got really upset that the dogmas of papal infallibility and papal primacy of jurisdiction were pushed through at Vatican I.

For me, the path to the Old Catholic Church[2] was obvious; it was simply a move from one Catholic diocese to another, much freer, one. Well, the paid pastoral positions in the Old Catholic diocese in Germany are few, and I wouldn't have been willing to go anywhere else. I threw myself into being a

---

2. The Old Catholic Church began in opposition to the First Vatican Council, which promulgated the doctrine of papal infallibility, although the roots of dissent were laid earlier in Utrecht. The See of Utrecht ordained priests and bishops for those Catholics in Germany, Austria-Hungary, and Switzerland who disagreed with Vatican I. Soon, they became their own denomination, not in communion with the Roman Catholic Church. The Old Catholic Church was and is more progressive than the official Roman Church, as it began using the vernacular in worship in the late nineteenth century and did away with clerical celibacy. Today, the Old Catholic Church ordains women and supports and affirms LGBTQIA+ people. There are around 115,000 Old Catholic faithful worldwide today.

"priest with a civil profession" as it was called at the time, and I volunteer as a pastor to this day. I love my somewhat alternative, Old Catholic congregation and have since grown together with the people.

When the state established registered domestic partnerships much later, Sepp and I also entered into this, with the blessing of our Church. We were together for a total of seventeen years until death parted us. And yes, I would do it all over again today. Because it was and is the way of love. And if "I do not have love, I am a noisy gong or a clanging cymbal" (1 Cor 13:1).

Three Days in Spring
Dr. Matthias Remenyi
(born in 1971, professor of fundamental theology)

The first day was on February 22, 2021. On this day, the note of the Congregation for the Doctrine of the Faith, published on March 15, 2021, forbidding the blessing of same-sex partnerships was signed. This date is certainly no coincidence. February 22 is the Feast of the *Cathedra Petri*, the feast of the Roman Magisterium itself. The very choice of the date shows that with this *responsum*, with this answer to a question of doubt, whoever submitted it, Rome makes it unmistakably clear who is in charge. It is by no means simply a question of whether these blessings are too closely related theologically and liturgically to the sacrament of marriage. Rather, it is about the validity of Catholic sexual morality, which rejects homosexuality as not being in accordance with creation. While the homosexual person is, of course, loved by God and therefore able to be blessed, the blessing of same-sex partnerships is impossible because the sexual acts performed in such a union are not to be approved but rather rejected as against God's will. But the distinction between person and act is untenable. After all, it is the center of the heart of the homosexual person, their whole love, their longing, and their innermost desire, which, when expressed, is condemned by the Church! This Church teaching is discriminatory. It needs to be changed. All official Church statements of appreciation toward lesbians, gays, and other queer people are smoke and mirrors as long as these stipulations remain.

My second day was Monday, March 22, 2021. Exactly one week after the *responsum* was published, a statement by professors of Catholic theology was posted online, which rejects the Roman text as discriminatory and expressly welcomes the blessing ceremonies it criticized. When it was first published, 212 people signed it, and now there are more than 280 cosignatories from German-speaking countries. I also signed it out of respect for my gay and lesbian colleagues, as well as those in the clergy. I signed it out of respect for homosexual people and couples, some of whom are close friends of mine. Finally, I signed it out of respect for my former colleague Ruben Schneider, who came out in an anthology on the MHG Study that I coedited.[1] He put it all out there on the page, both biographically and scientifically. The protest from theologians was important, first, of course, as a display of solidarity. Ultimately, it is about the question of where the Church stands on human rights, specifically on the right to personal integrity and sexual self-determination.

The third day was on May 10, 2021. On this day, despite the Roman ban, such blessing services were held throughout Germany under the motto #lovewins. Even the Augustinian Church in Würzburg took part. I also took part, and I was

---

1. The Mannheim-Heidelberg-Giessen Study (named after the universities of the main researchers) was a study of clerical sexual abuse in Germany. It was carried out from 2014 to 2018 and involved scholars and researchers of mental health, criminology, and other disciplines. The final report is titled *Sexueller Missbrauch an Minderjährigen durch katholische Priester, Diakone und männliche Ordensangehörige im Bereich der Deutschen Bischofskonferenz* ("Sexual Abuse of Minors by Catholic Priests, Deacons, and Religious in the Jurisdiction of the German Bishops' Conference"). The anthology the author refers to is Matthias Remenyi and Thomas Schärtl, eds., *Nicht ausweichen: Theologie angesichts der Missbrauchskrise* (Regensburg: Friedrich Pustet, 2019).

Three Days in Spring

deeply moved. Because, despite all the prophecies of doom, love actually won that day. In front of me sat an elderly couple, together, I suspected, with their son and son-in-law. They were so proud of each other, so happy with each other, and happy being here together. Love had won. At least on this day, in this place. And me? I thought of my wife, who was in bed with a migraine, of the path we walked together and of what may still lie ahead of us. Then I went up to one of the ministers, dutifully stood in line, and when it was my turn, I asked for the blessing.

My Lesbian Daughter Can Be Sure of My Love and of God's Love

Katrin Richthofer
(born in 1970, director and event manager)

My (step)daughter, Cosima, announced at the age of fifteen that she was "definitely not straight." Fortunately, she was aware that no announcement in the world would change our love for her the slightest bit. "You are loved—just as you are and feel!"

For as long as she can remember, the Catholic Church has been a second home to her. She is now a senior acolyte and has completed her JuLeiCa[1] so she can work with children: a model Catholic. So far. With the latest ban from the Vatican on blessing same-sex couples, however, it was official: her God-given ability to experience love is sinful for the Catholic Church.

---

1. The *Jugendleiter*in-Card* (*Juleica*, sometimes *JuLeiCa*) is a federal ID certifying one in voluntary youth work. It requires thirty to fifty hours of training, including how to perform tasks and lead groups, aims and methods, legal and organizational issues, psychological and educational basics, and recognizing signs of endangerment. It is valid for three years, and a cardholder must complete further training to renew their Juleica.

My Lesbian Daughter Can Be Sure of My Love

Not being straight was already a big challenge for her. "How would family and friends react?" "How would I be able to start a long-awaited family someday?" "Which countries should I avoid if I want to go on vacation with my partner?" And then some Catholics from Rome tell her that her form of love is sinful.

After her parents divorced, she experienced a very different way of dealing with violations in the Catholic Church. When her father sat down with her in his usual seat in the church, his pew-neighbors, who had sat next to him for years, just had to ask why they didn't move away. So, she only dared to hope for limited "grace" anyway.

Being Catholic and being LGBTQIA+ today is certainly not a particularly rewarding combination. My response to her concerns was very practical. As a member of Mary 2.0,[2] I helped organize a #lovewins worship service. It was a wonderful service and simultaneously a clear sign to everyone who participated and to Cosima, saying, "You are a blessing!"

What was frightening for me, however, were the threats and insults that were made in the days building up to the #lovewins service and then afterward as a reaction to it: "You will pay for this," "You let Satan into the church," and so on. Experienced homosexuals dismissed these, saying, "That happens all the time!"

Since then, there have been many more talks with Cosi. I wanted to give her arguments and at least to be able to intercept the ignorant, unintentional aggressions. "No, the repeatedly quoted Bible texts are not about homosexual love." What else can I do? Love unconditionally! Always give Cosi a hug when a stupid comment comes up somewhere. And, of course, fight for a change, at least for the Catholic Church in Germany!

---

2. See "Catholic Means Universal and That Includes Everyone," note 1.

Queerness IN THE Catholic Church

Why do I, myself, the daughter of a religious teacher, an *Altcusanerin*,³ and a member of *ND*,⁴ want to remain Catholic? Because I am Catholic still—despite divorce, despite exclusion, despite many abuses. Because I have always met wonderful people who have made Church my home. I see it as my mission to give as many people as possible the chance to experience Church as home (again), no matter who they are, how they feel, or how they have failed.

That's the message I want to give to Cosi: "Don't let a Church destroy your faith! God created you exactly as you are and loves you unconditionally! Be always sure of God's love and my love! And (responsibly) follow the path that you believe will bring love and joy into your life and the lives of others! Period."

---

3. The *Cusanuswerk* is a sponsorship and scholarship program for gifted Catholic high school and college students who demonstrate excellence in academics, social engagement, and Catholic identity. Recipients of the *Cusanuswerk* awards are called *Altcusaner*innen*.

4. *ND-Christsein.heute*, "ND-Christianity.today" (formerly the *Bund Neudeutschland*), often *ND*, is a Catholic association with an emphasis on social and political engagement within the Church and society, often in support of progressive issues.

God Called Me to Be Gay and a Priest

Anonymous
(born in 1965, priest and publicist)

I am a priest. And I am gay. I don't see either as a contradiction. On the contrary, for me, both belong together. I am both; both are what I am. And that's why I don't want to be anything other than what I am. It feels good and right that I am a priest; it feels good and right that I am gay. I firmly believe both come from God, both are willed by God, both show how God wants me and what God wants from me. Both are my calling.

That's why I see both as grace, as a gift, if not as a privilege—but not in the sense that I pride myself on it. Ultimately, neither were the result of my own will and actions, but they came from the will and actions of God. I didn't choose to be a priest and I didn't choose to be gay. However, I still regard both as a privilege because God's providence, God's trust, and God's love are expressed in both.

Therefore, I'm at peace with God and I'm at peace with myself. I'm not, however, at peace with the Church. Because if it were up to the Church, I shouldn't even be a priest. Although I was already a priest at the time, I was angered, disturbed, and hurt when the Congregation for Catholic Education issued an instruction on November 4, 2005, stating that the Church "cannot admit to…holy orders those who…present deep-seated homosexual tendencies."[1]

The instruction attempts to justify that gay men should not be allowed to become priests or, if they are already priests, actually shouldn't be by saying, "One must in no way overlook the negative consequences that can derive from the ordination of persons with deep-seated homosexual tendencies."[2] This is not a justification, however, but merely a declaration, and an empty declaration at that, since the instruction does not provide any information about what these allegedly negative consequences are.

If this assertion were true, then these negative consequences should be obvious and exist now in the work of all the gay priests and, presumably, have always existed. Serious estimates assume that one-third to well over half of Catholic priests are gay.[3] Although it is hard to dispute that the work of some priests has had negative consequences, this is by no means true only for gay priests, and none of this is the direct consequence of their being gay.

With its unfounded claim that the ordination of gay people has negative consequences, the Church tramples on the lifetime of achievements of every gay priest that has ever existed. It gives gay priests the painful feeling that they shouldn't be who they are. And it has discouraged some gay men called to the priesthood from following their calling. It is

---

1. Congregation for Catholic Education, "Instruction Concerning the Criteria for the Discernment of Vocations with regard to Persons with Homosexual Tendencies in View of Their Admission to the Seminary and to Holy Orders," November 4, 2005, no. 2.

2. Congregation for Catholic Education, "Instruction Concerning the Criteria for the Discernment of Vocations," n. 2.

3. See Elizabeth Dias, "'It Is Not a Closet. It Is a Cage': Gay Catholic Priests Speak Out," The New York Times, February 17, 2019, https://www.nytimes.com/2019/02/17/us/it-is-not-a-closet-it-is-a-cage-gay-catholic-priests-speak-out.html.

not the ordination of gay men that has negative consequences but, on the contrary, their rejection.

Still, I sometimes wonder if, as a gay man, I should be a priest. I ask myself this, even though I know that God has called me to be both a priest and a gay man, and I enjoy being both. I ask myself this because it is becoming increasingly difficult for me to bear witness to and work for a Church that continually vilifies, unsettles, and hurts people like me. Why do I continue? Maybe to prove a gay man being a priest doesn't just have negative consequences.

I Lived behind a Mask for a Long Time

Anonymous
(born in 1970, doctor)

I am a Catholic trans woman. Only recently was my transgender identity officially established. Until then, I was in transition. In my native Poland, trans people are treated as second-class citizens. The Catholic Church is to blame for this.

My negative experiences with the Catholic Church began in my early teens. When I started preschool, I couldn't speak yet. Because of this, I was often beaten by the religious sisters who ran the preschool.

I have hidden my otherness as a transgender person behind a mask since my childhood. I lived in constant fear that it might come out. In my fear, I kept praying to God for help. I felt intense guilt for a long time. I thought that being different was a punishment from God, but I didn't know why.

The Church was no help—in fact, quite the contrary. My otherness was either not taken seriously, or it was seen as a perversion. "You'll get over it," I heard repeatedly in confession. To help me get over it, some priests imposed particularly severe penances on me.

I Lived behind a Mask for a Long Time

After publicizing my trans identity, priests and members of my Catholic community kept telling me, "You shouldn't be here! You don't belong here! This isn't the place for you!" Because the Catholic Church rejects my identity as transgender, so do my own parents—even to this day.

In my native Poland, the climate is extremely hostile toward LGBTQIA+ issues, not only in society, but especially in the Catholic Church. Many priests run a regular anti-LGBTQIA+ campaign. They hang posters with anti-LGBTQIA+ slogans in their community bulletin boards. They openly promote anti-LGBTQIA+, nationalist, and right-wing positions in their sermons. Many of my friends who feel discriminated against and hurt because of their membership in the LGBTQIA+ community have now left the Church. Some of them are understandably unfavorable, if not hostile, to the Church.

But I am still Catholic and would like to remain so, because the Catholic faith is very important to me. Unfortunately, in the Church I'm not allowed to be myself—the person who I really am. I feel discriminated against, marginalized, and rejected.

Still, I'm not giving up hope that God can soften the hardened hearts of anti-LGBTQIA+ people. And so, I pray often, "Send forth your spirit, they are created; and you renew the face of the [earth]" (Ps 104:30). I especially hope that God will also renew the face of the earth in my native Poland!

The Church Rejects Me as Trans— My Parish Doesn't

Cleo Schmitz
(born in 1970, information technology teacher)

It took me a long time to understand that I'm trans.

I was active in our parish and a member of the local municipal council when I began to be open about being a woman to those around me. Before that, I had thought long and hard about what that might mean for my situation in the community and parish.

When I spoke to our pastor about this, his main question was, "What does your family say about it, your wife, and your children?" I explained to him that I had already spoken to them and that neither they nor I needed any pastoral counseling. That settled the matter for him; people who love and support one another, and are concerned for one another, is not a problem that he needs to interfere in.

My conversation with the mayor was similar. I agreed to step down from my position on the council if there were any problems. Her reaction was unequivocal, "Cleo, the community didn't choose you as a man or a woman, but as a person."

The Church Rejects Me as Trans—My Parish Doesn't

All of these reactions led to my willingness in September 2020 to tell the entire local council that I am a trans woman. As a result of the coronavirus pandemic and the applicable distance rules, the meeting did not take place in the community hall as usual, but in the church. And because we also wanted to talk about topics that affected the parish, around fifty people were present instead of the twelve members of the municipal council.

The meetings of the municipal council are open to the public. And so, I stood in front with a microphone in hand and I asked myself: "What should I say?"

Luckily, I had enough time to think beforehand. I wondered whether there were perhaps any understanding statements on the part of the Church on trans identity. Maybe Pope Francis had said something positive about it. But the more I learned about the Church's official position, the more worried I became. For example, I read, "Pope Condemns Transgender Ideology." From the official point of view of the Church, my realization that I can only continue my life as a woman is "a decision that carries the risk of endangering the relationship between man and woman."[1] If someone from the parish had read that, I thought, then I wouldn't be able to show up there again.

But why am I even doing all this to myself? The Church and my parish have always been the focus of my social life, as an acolyte, as a member of Catholic youth groups, in the context of confirmation catechesis, in the circle of eucharistic ministers and lectors, and currently in the parish council. Would I have to give up all this and the opportunity to live my life authentically? There was no other option; I would have to find out.

---

1. I suspect this primarily refers to the Congregation for Catholic Education's document, "'Male and Female He Created Them'" although I am unable to find the exact quote.

Queerness IN THE Catholic Church

Luckily, my coming out was well-received in the parish. I received a lot of encouragement and support. If someone from the parish accidentally or intentionally addresses me with the wrong gender, I can count on the person in question being corrected quickly and sensitively by others—often even faster than I can react myself."That's *Mrs*. Schmitz!" I am very grateful for that.

When No One Can Hear You Scream

Dr. Ruben Schneider
(born in 1978, research assistant)

I'm gay and Catholic. I am a survivor of physical abuse from homophobic Catholic teachings. For example, in the October 1, 1986, letter of the Congregation for the Doctrine of the Faith "On the Pastoral Care of Homosexual Persons,"[1] homosexual acts are condemned as an "objective disorder" and intrinsic evil. Accordingly, the homosexual disposition, regardless of its actual expression, is considered an "objectively disordered inclination." That is, for the magisterium, the homosexual orientation itself is an orientation toward an intrinsic evil. In the innermost part of one's own soul, the involuntary desire for evil constantly festers. The noblest desire, love, turns into the most terrible thing, into the deepest abyss of separation from God.

In Catholic socialization, this condemnation of the innermost emotional life of homosexual people can have an effect

---

1. Congregation for the Doctrine of Faith, "Letter to the Bishops of the Catholic Church on the Pastoral Care of Homosexual Persons," October 1, 1986, https://www.vatican.va/roman_curia/congregations/cfaith/documents/rc_con_cfaith_doc_19861001_homosexual-persons_en.html.

Queerness IN THE Catholic Church

on adolescents who are attracted to the same sex, even before their homosexuality fully awakens. They internalize the taboo of such teaching unquestioningly and unconsciously before they can even defend themselves against it. That's what I did. I found my innermost being to be wrong, gross, unnatural, and disgusting. Something to be kept secret. Love and self-love were replaced by toxic self-loathing, guilt, and shame. This is called internalized homophobia in psychological jargon. Internalized homophobia causes deep developmental disorders in teenagers; the young person's identity formation and self-realization is disrupted during a crucial phase of maturation. A healthy and authentic relationship with oneself doesn't develop. This can become a trauma carved deeply into one's very nervous system and continues to have an effect throughout adulthood. Most LGBTQIA+ youth have never been able to experience authentic love; all love, even that of their parents, has not reached their authentic selves. The long-term consequences can be manifold.

In this inner emptiness and in the outer isolation of an environment that makes homosexuality taboo, nobody hears you scream. I was alone. I was broken inside; I couldn't make it to school anymore. A cascade of failed classes followed, until at some point, out of sheer defiance, I took my *Abitur*[2] off-campus, which I barely managed to pass.

Pious as I was, I then wanted to join a religious order. However, the admission process included a psychological test, which, among other things, was to use special methods to check whether you were homosexual. It was the time of the first abuse scandals in the United States. After the Church had taught me all my life to hide and hate my sexual orientation, a "gay test" was suddenly threatening me with an involuntary and cold exposure. This was all physical violence. It shattered

---

2. The *Abitur* is a finishing exam for high school required to graduate. This is like the *Matura* or the A-Levels in the UK.

my fragile coping mechanisms and caused a severe anxiety disorder with suicidal tendencies.

To this day, this phase of life still causes me to suffer. The fact that I managed to finish school and now work as a research assistant is almost a miracle. Looking toward the future, I wish for a clear end to discrimination and for priests, theologians, and Church workers not simply to use LGBTQIA+ issues for symbolic activism or for political self-promotion, but for us all to create a Church environment through everyday hard work, an environment in which everyone can stand up for themselves. Because that's the only way we can conquer the isolation of taboo.

Quo Vadis?

Anonymous
(born in 1980, church musician)

Some readers probably think of the impressive 1951 film with Sir Peter Ustinov in the role of Emperor Nero, or the legend that underlies this film's title when Peter, wanting to escape from Rome and his pursuers, met Jesus, whom he asked in astonishment, "*Domine, quo vadis?*" In English, "Lord, where are you going?" Jesus is said to have replied, "I am going to Rome to be crucified again," which Peter understood as an invitation to turn around and face martyrdom.

When I was asked to write a contribution for this book, I agreed immediately and enthusiastically. But then when I got into it, when I had to get into myself, it became difficult. Long-forgotten wounds resurfaced. As I wrote, I needed to work through a now thirty-year-long path, paved with fear, hide-and-seek, and inner turmoil. Perhaps this is reflected latently in these lines. Do I have the courage to publish this article under my name? No, we haven't gotten that far here in the country and in the various parishes where I work.

"*Quo vadis?*" I've been asking myself that question every day since I was young. In other words, "How far do you go?" How far do I let the people entrusted to me in choirs and groups into my personal life? At what point am I putting my career on the line?

Quo Vadis?

The fact is I exist, and I only exist once. I am who God created me to be with all my flaws and weaknesses but also with my own talents and abilities. Can I compartmentalize myself and disguise who I am? No, I can't do that. As I get older, I don't want to do that anymore. When I make music, I do it as the person I am. Can the organ sound gay? That's absurd!

Nevertheless, I have hidden myself, my thoughts, my feelings, my longings for many years. Day after day. Out of worry—because I don't want to lose what I love and what I live for—church music. This inner strife, these worries, and these fears cannot be bottled up.

Nevertheless, it's an open secret that I'm gay. Some know it, many suspect it, but nobody talks about it. But I am tolerated and accepted. The main thing is that the organ plays and the choir sings. But what about the person behind the organ and the choir?

I love and live for church music; it has been my vocation since childhood. I love the Catholic High Mass with all its mysticism, the pomp at festal Masses, everything that a good and dignified liturgy has to offer, but also the modest, almost intimate weekday Mass with few visitors. I love the special times of the liturgical year, especially Holy Week with such an intense celebration of Christ's passion, death, and resurrection.

But do I—the person I am—really belong? Why did God give me musical talent while also giving me the stigma of homosexuality? "*Quo vadis?*" I ask myself too. I wish that Mother Church could be a real mother who loves all her children, like my parents, who were not thrilled when I came out to them (much too late), but who still love, accept, support, and encourage me. If the Church did the same, it would be on the right path—the path that Jesus showed us: the path of love.

My Gay "Little" Brother
Dr. Thomas Schüller
(born in 1961, professor of canon law)

I come from a large Catholic family—four brothers and one sister, who has sadly passed away. We still love calling my youngest brother the little one, despite being fifty-five years old. He is gay and has been living with my favorite Catholic brother-in-law for over thirty years. They were in a civil partnership, then upgraded to being married. More questions? Well, with a father born in 1919, who was a product of his time and thought conservatively, it took a long time before our brother was able to talk openly about his homosexuality and his partner. My widowed mother needed our pastor's wise counsel in dealing with this situation. Today, she wouldn't know what to do without our brother-in-law's empathetic and loving care. In her old age, her everyday life is becoming more difficult, and he supports us brothers more than enthusiastically in our care of our elderly mother. He has become her fifth son and our brother.

Why am I explaining this? Well, when Bishop Franz Kamphaus was looking for a contact person for the "Project: Gay and Catholic in the Parish of Our Lady Help of Christians"[1] in Frankfurt, which still exists today, he approached me as his canon lawyer and personal advisor. Sure, how many times

---

1. See "The Beam in the Eye," note 1.

My Gay "Little" Brother

have we had to answer Cardinal Ratzinger's concerned letters about the purity of Catholic sexual morality and, above all, the holy liturgy in the diocese of Limburg because of written denunciations of this project by supposedly model conservative Catholics in Rome? But my bishop sent me to this project with the suggestion that I was already familiar with these Christians through my brother. To this day, I feel closely connected to all the comrades-in-arms from that time in Frankfurt in this project, who provided, then and now, a spiritual home for gay and lesbian Catholics. On August 29, 2021, the main Catholic church in Frankfurt awarded one of the founders of this project, Georg Trettin, its highest award, the Bartholomew Plaque. One might think that gay Catholics have arrived at the center of the Church.

Unfortunately, that's not true. Gay and lesbian Catholics, even in otherwise liberal Catholic milieus, are still met with suspicion and concerns. The truly innocent, and yet so powerful, demand for the blessing of same-sex couples right now is countered with the absurd "argument" that one does not want to endanger the ideal of heterosexual marriage. In a Church and society that, despite its ostentatiously flaunted liberality, is still deeply defined by a gender-binary model of sexuality. Thus, homophobic resentment piles up, just waiting for a spark to make it burst into flames. Hungary[2] or Georgia[3] should be our cautionary tales.

And regarding canon law: it establishes the framework for magisterial decisions such as that gay men may not be

---

2. In 2021, Hungary passed a law that bans "promoting" LGBTQIA+ information to minors as part of its "Anti-Pedophilia Act." See, e.g., https://www.dw.com/en/hungarys-anti-lgbtq-law-comes-into-effect/a-58198511.

3. Georgia's first Pride march was to take place on July 5, 2021, but was disrupted by far-right mobs. In the following days, LGBTQIA+ people faced violent physical attacks and harassment, causing many to flee. Georgia is considered one of the most homophobic countries in Europe. See, e.g., https://oc-media.org/features/datablog-georgia-may-be-the-most-homophobic-country-in-europe/.

Queerness IN THE Catholic Church

ordained priests or face a summons if they marry a couple even though state law allows it. State law that still applies and cannot be done away with by cheap Sunday speeches. Canon law makes it doctrine to obey state laws, so this takes bold steps to change Catholic doctrine. Pity, tact, and sensitivity are no longer enough. Gay and lesbian Catholics live out the love of God, which is morally good, in their enduring relationships. They are created in the image of God, and they are our sisters and brothers—without any exception.

Doubt, Love, and the Incomplete Basilica of St. Peter

Martin Speer
(born in 1986, author and policy adviser)

"How can you even think about becoming a Catholic—you of all people as a gay man and a self-proclaimed feminist?" I hear this question again and again whenever I speak, publicly or privately, about how deeply the Christian faith and the Catholic Church touch me. But maybe it's because I am who I am that things fit so well together. And indeed, far more than I would like to concede to myself, let alone the Church: I'm on my way to becoming Catholic.

All of this is no coincidence. Faith and the Church have had a deep fascination for me since my early childhood. Even though I grew up in a Protestant environment, it's still the Catholic Church—its tradition, teaching, liturgy, and way of life—that touches both my heart and my head. It's hard to put into words what I'm feeling. But if I had to break it down to three words, they would be: Love, Peace, and Movement. I feel deeply loved by God, I find peace in the Church and community, and at the same time, I am encouraged to move toward progress and growth.

But it is precisely that last point that sets me at odds with the Church and distances me from it. How can the leaders of an institution based on faith that demands a disposition toward progress, humility, and self-reflection from us all (still) fail so much in applying these attributes themselves? How can Catholic teaching that, on the one hand, inspires spiritual growth and charity simultaneously serve as a fig leaf for the continuation of a practice based on devaluing and discriminating against homosexuals, women, and other groups of people? The all-encompassing love that we see in the ministry of Jesus Christ, in the lives of the many saints, and in the hundreds of thousands of committed people within the Church still is not adequately expressed in its doctrine. These contradictions hurt, and with each passing day, they take away the credibility and soul of the Church.

But will that stop me from becoming a Catholic one day? No. Because today I see on every corner a Church that is more queer, more feminist, and more progressive than it would like to admit. We just need to open our eyes. I see clergy blessing gay couples, women taking over more and more spaces, and millions of believers around the world ready for a great progressive leap in Catholic teaching. I have hope that the Church will find its way back to where it came from. Back to the future, so to speak. It was born out of God's love for people and grew up in the love of people for one another. Love takes the lead, and therefore nothing else can happen, nothing else will happen except that one day this love will embrace everything and everyone. Even those of us who are still on the fringes today.

Don't Be Afraid of Change

Andreas Sturm
(born in 1974, priest and vicar general)

I still remember that Monday in March when the message popped up on my cell phone. The Congregation for the Doctrine of the Faith decided to ban blessing ceremonies for same-sex couples. I was stunned. So many people came to mind: the lesbian couple whose children I had baptized and who had been living together for many years, or the gay friend who, after going through a difficult time, was now thriving in a relationship with a man.

At this point, my training in clinical pastoral care in New York proved formative for me. I had worked in a hospice for AIDS patients. At the request of the dying, we tried to contact family members so that they could say goodbye to each other. But I've seen several parents claiming that they no longer have a child, only after repeated inquiries to declare that "this queer" is no longer their child. They weren't all Catholics, but it became clear from the conversations that everyone considered themselves to be particularly good Christians, leaving only us chaplains to stay with them at the bedside until their last breath.

Queerness IN THE Catholic Church

But there were always good experiences. However, I never saw myself as an advocate or activist. I've celebrated blessings before, but behind closed doors and only for the couple themselves. I did it because I felt it was spiritually and pastorally necessary, and I would do it again for any couple. But today I am ashamed of having celebrated blessing services alone with the couple in the church, without relatives, family, or friends. I was afraid of trouble and disagreements.

All of this went through my head and made me increasingly restless, robbing me of sleep. I always celebrate Mass on Tuesday mornings with a religious community, as I did the day after the letter from the Congregation for the Doctrine of the Faith was published. In the stillness after communion, I was filled with the certainty that I can no longer be guided by fears. Shortly thereafter, I posted my thoughts on Facebook: "I have blessed apartments, cars, elevators, countless rosaries, and so on, and I shouldn't bless two people who love each other? That can't be God's will."

It wasn't long before the phone rang with newspapers, radio, and television reporters. The reactions in the days and weeks that followed were overwhelming. What touched me most were the letters from parents who wanted to live their Catholic faith but at the same time wanted to stand by their children who had come out. There were also notes from lesbian and gay people who, when they came out, wished for a Church that not only "accept[s] with respect, compassion, and sensitivity"[1] but also appreciates that their love for a man or woman is a gift from God. Of course, there were also negative reactions that were very emotional, but overall, they hardly carried any weight.

In almost two thousand years, the Church has repeatedly asked itself new questions about new topics. We are currently

---

1. CCC 2358.

Don't Be Afraid of Change

doing this in Germany as part of the Synodal Path. God's liberating Spirit and not fear of change must be our leitmotif. As a Church, we should not prevent discussion in a *basta!* mentality.[2] Every human being, without exception, is made in the image of God, and perhaps we just haven't fully understood what God's Spirit wants to convey to his Church through his beloved homosexual daughters and sons.

---

2. Italian, now German slang, for "That's enough!"

Homophobia in God's Name Is Spiritual Abuse

Anonymous
(born in 2000, student)

A few days ago, I met a young man my age—in the usual way (at least these days), via a dating app. He had messaged me a few times before and kept asking me out on a date, but it didn't happen for a while because I initially kept turning him down.

Finally, one evening, I agreed. He came to my place, and, after a few minutes, it was like we had known each other for years. We talked, laughed at each other's jokes, and had a lot of fun together. It felt like home in my heart. There was that certain something when we looked at each other. When I reflect on it, the butterflies in my stomach just start fluttering again....

My time with him was like a dream I didn't want to wake up from, but inevitably I eventually did. Our encounter, a moment of the deepest happiness, was taken over by irrational fear: fear that it was just a dream; fear that something wasn't right; fear that something would end before it even really began.

This fear—the fear that something can't be because something says it's not allowed—is the most torment I've ever felt. It feels like you've lost something you haven't even gained yet. These vicious, paralyzing thoughts haunt me during the day, in my sleep, in everything.

But why? Because deep in my subconscious, deep in my heart, there's still that fog that's wafting up, a fog that rises every time someone I really like comes into my life. For a long time, I believed that being gay wasn't okay. I thought being gay was wrong, so I could never be happy if I allowed myself to live gay. The jokes that were told about being gay in school, the ingrained hatred of gay people in society and in my family, and the Church's official position on homosexuality all played a part in shaping me.

Today I'm out, but within my family I'm still considered straight. After my mother found out that I was gay, she made me promise her that I would keep this secret within the family. Even after all the humiliation and insults, I feel sorrier today for my mother. Because she abuses faith itself when she says that I shouldn't do something so deviant and sick and instead must bear my gay feelings like a cross. God thinks it's deviant if a man has a relationship with a man, let alone have sex with him.

Why do so many people claim that they know exactly what God wants and doesn't want? How are believing parents supposed to stand behind their queer children if the Church doesn't stand behind them? And more important, how are young queer believers supposed to commit to the Church if the Church doesn't commit to them?

I firmly believe in my heart that God is good and kind. Maybe my family doesn't support me the way I wish they would. But I will not let my faith in God be taken from me,

Queerness IN THE Catholic Church

whatever happened and whatever will come. God will always be with me, giving me strength and joy. I am grateful for that.

I experienced what God really is like when I was with the young man I wrote about earlier—my fear decreased after I prayed for God's guidance.

Telling My Lesbian Daughter That Being a Catholic Is Liberating

Christian Taufenbach
(born in 1966, architect)

Growing up as a Rhenish[1] Catholic, in the best sense of the term, is a lesson from my mother that was burned deep into my life. When I complained to her about some authority figure who had disciplined me, she said, "No matter what a minister, a policeman, a teacher may say to you, your own conscience is always supreme. Don't let anyone tell you otherwise. You have my permission to follow it, and you should." She said that as a matter of faith. Through many years of life within the Church, as an altar server, cantor, parish and deanery council member, in *Cusanuswerk* and *ND*,[2] I carried the conviction that being Catholic above all strengthens one's freedom.

I became even more aware of the force of the advice from my mother over the course of my life, experiencing various breaks and natural endings, especially when my first marriage failed. As a result of separation, divorce, and remarriage, I had

---
1. A native of Rhineland, stereotypically Catholic (and often conservative).
2. See "My Lesbian Daughter Can Be Sure of My Love," notes 3 and 4.

to experience what it means to be criticized by people who think they are holier than thou. Mind you, rather than the parish staff, it was the angry voices from the parish who only have a (small) measure of sense (*gewissermassen*) who tried to remove me—how apt is that word.³

Unfortunately, our pastor could not find the words to build the necessary bridge. Being singled out from my own community that I had poured so much heart and soul into caused a deep cut that lets me keep my distance today. In the Alpine Club, you can freely engage with ideology, which is nice.⁴ Nevertheless, evening-long debates with friends about the innermost working that believers in the Church could have together, conversations with our seven children about our own faith and occasionally deep joy in the high moments of the liturgy, they still exist. But an indelible "Leave me alone!" keeps me from getting involved in our Church as I used to.

And then my fifteen-year-old daughter confided in me that she was "at least bi." A few months later, she felt able to speak more freely; today she is a self-confident lesbian, with eyes open for love and everything else fitting for a young person who knows who they are. I realized that my Catholic code at this point, while theoretically liberal, was too abstract. This maturing girl challenged me to take a stance. The whole range of reflexes washed up in my mind, "You have to fight against

---

3. This is difficult for me to translate. *Wohlgemerkt waren es eher lautstarke Menschen aus der Gemeinde als hauptamtliche Mitarbeiter*innen, die danach trachteten, mich gewissermaßen – wie treffend ist diese Wort – zu entfernen.* I see two possibilities: (1) *gewissermaßen:* "in a sense," perhaps literally "a measure of sense," referring to the fact that the angry voices from the parish only have a [small] measure of sense at all; (2) *entfernen:* "removal" may be translated less commonly as "deletion," "elimination," or "get rid of," which may carry connotations of violence implying the darkest end of such attitudes.

4. The *Deutscher Alpineverein* is a mountaineering organization that promotes hiking and mountaineering, while also promoting conservation, inclusion, and diversity.

it, then it will be fine," "It's just nature"—none of this fit my mother's sentence about conscience.

The conversations with my daughter became deeper over time. Today, they revolve around the question of how she can find a home in a Church in which offenses against queer people occur so openly or are just barely hidden under pious vestments. I don't understand the use of biblical clobber-verses to portray something as an abomination that is an inherent part of creation. And I know from my own failed experience that it's not just a question of will for a person to adjust their path, especially when it seems like the correct path according to the Church. I want to give her what keeps me in dialectic relationship with the Church to this day: being a Catholic is liberating, because God's mercy is inexhaustible.

Or to put it in the words of a priest friend, who, for a long time as a child, wondered what on earth this threatening and penetrating eye of God, as portrayed in many churches, is supposed to mean, "At some point it became clear to me: God's winking with the other eye straight at me." And that man is Westphalian.[5]

---

[5]. Regional cultures and the meanings attached to them are difficult to translate, but Westphalia is in the same region as Rhineland, where the author grew up. I will suggest that Westphalians are known as cheerful and hard-working, based on a travel article from DW.com. Elisabeth Yorck von Wartenburg, "10 Reasons to Love North Rhine-Westphalia," DW, April 6, 2019, https://www.dw.com/en/10-reasons-to-love-north-rhine-westphalia/g-18354998.

Hoping for a Miracle
Stefan Theierl
(born in 1978, palliative care nurse)

I grew up in the Allgäu. My family is nominally Catholic, but we rarely went to church. Nevertheless, I had a strong relationship with religion and God as a child. My spirituality as a child was very positive—full of love and trust.

My spirituality was first dampened by an aunt who practiced a more somber version of faith. She taught me that it is very difficult to get to heaven and that God is above all an angry, punishing God. I can still recall those gloomy images of the Crucified One on Mount Golgotha today.

The local pastor taught religion at my school. He was a good storyteller but relentlessly pursued the children who failed to show up for Sunday services and pursued them with extreme psychological control. His explanations about how God would punish people's transgressions were very vivid; we even had pictures of hell to color in. Soon my relationship with God was no longer so relaxed.

When my sexuality awakened during puberty, it turned out to be a rude awakening. It soon became clear to me that I was homosexual, and I already knew what that meant from a Catholic perspective. I lived in terrible fear and shame for years, trying to hide my sexual identity and hoping for a miracle. I led a double life. A first kiss, being in love as a teenager,

Hoping for a Miracle

adolescent flirtations, or even just holding hands with a crush were reserved for others—never for me. This conflict became so great that I left the Church as a young adult. Despite everything, doing so was still very difficult for me, because although I had broken with this dark side of Catholicism, the fear of damnation remained with me. Although, I still had strong spiritual desires. I fulfilled these with yoga, Buddhism, and modern esotericism. I spent many years trying to rebuild my image of God through the lens of the different world religions and more.

I was denied a happy, loving relationship, and in my mid-thirties, a crisis shook me; I felt like the rug was pulled out from under my feet. Despite this—or perhaps because of this—I was able to have a strong spiritual experience. Just like when I was a child, I felt that old, loving, and benevolent relationship with God. A love that is bestowed without conditions, very near, and without any question. The nearness of God was complete and strong; it felt certain.

I felt a sincere desire to rejoin the Church; this time without fear and as the person I really am. I addressed this and my sexual identity during my conversation about rejoining the Church with my pastor. I made it clear that I will stand up for myself and never want to see any of this portrayed as sin again. To my surprise, this pastor validated me and spoke of being appreciative for every love. He suggested that I always read the Bible in its historical context and to always see God as the God of love.

As if by a miracle, my life changed. I soon met my husband, and we have been living together happily ever since. We attend worship services together and enjoy a wonderful, loving spirituality that carries us through life and fills us anew every day.

I am still critical of the Catholic Church. How could it be changed? For me, however, this loving, benevolent God is above this Church whose failings I cannot accept uncritically. Therefore, my faith is stronger.

Faith Is a Part of Who I Am—Just Like Being Gay

Stefan Thurner
(born in 1992, elder caregiver)

The Catholic faith and the Catholic Church have been part of my life since childhood. I was particularly influenced by my mother, who used to work in a monastery, and by my maternal grandparents, who often took me to church services. After my first communion, I became an altar server—a ministry that I continue with enthusiasm today. I've also been a lector for many years.

I would have liked to work for the Church. I could even have imagined studying theology and becoming a priest. It wasn't just the fact that I didn't pass my *Abitur*;[1] I could have picked that up somehow. The main argument against it was being gay. Ever since adolescence, I knew that I liked men. And I also knew that the Catholic Church rejects gay priests. So, for better or for worse, I realized that a job within the Church would not work out.

---

1. See "When No One Can Hear You Scream," note 2.

Faith Is a Part of Who I Am—Just Like Being Gay

Instead, I became an elder caregiver. For me, this job is still somewhat of a pastoral profession. I can make life easier for people who need help and care. I try to assure them that their life still has meaning despite advanced age or illness. I can give them attention and show appreciation. I can listen to them, talk to them, and, when everything has been said, be silent with them too.

In my professional environment, it doesn't matter that I'm gay; in my church environment, it doesn't really matter either. On the one hand, this is good, but it's a shame, on the other. I can talk to our pastors[2] about anything, including being gay, but in parish life, the topic doesn't come up. Most people in the parish probably know I'm gay, but almost nobody talks about it. The topic is kept secret and suppressed—and a part of me with it.

The Church's official stance on sexual morality is to blame for this. Even though the topic doesn't arise in parish life, that is only because the subject of sexuality is completely taboo. The Church also marginalizes people—namely, everyone who is different and does not live according to the Church's official sexual morality: the remarried and divorced, for example, but also gay people.

Although I have no problems in my parish, and I feel welcome and accepted there just the way I am, I would like to see queer life in the Church become more visible. Pretending that queer people don't exist is just out of touch with reality. My ever-growing impression is that the Church lives in a world of illusion: both the Vatican, which does not want to admit that many people were created by God who the traditional image of sexuality, marriage, and family does not apply to; and the local congregations, who act as if the Church's official sexual morality does not exist.

---

2. *Seelsorgerinnen und Seelsorgern*, both female and male pastors are specified in the original.

Queerness IN THE Catholic Church

Still, leaving the Church is out of the question for me. I need the Church, I need the community of my parish, and I need the regular celebration of the Eucharist. The Catholic faith, and therefore also the Catholic Church, is a part of my life, a part of me—just like being gay.

Encounter Creates Change

Heinrich Timmerevers
(born in 1952, bishop of Dresden-Meissen)

One day, a group of queer Christians from Dresden asked if they could meet with me for a chat. I was unsure at first. What questions and concerns would these people have? How should I answer them? How can I face them? How do I address the hurts they have undoubtedly sustained throughout their lives? Nevertheless, I agreed to meet.

When they finally stood in front of me, I discovered, to my surprise, that I already knew several of them. I had only recently confirmed a man who used to live as a woman. I knew several others, or at least recognized them, from services in the Dresden cathedral. Thus, I was far less self-conscious about the encounter than I had feared. It was important to me that they felt welcome in the bishop's house. We had set up a large table where we served them a tasty meal with good wine.

What they had to tell me touched me deeply. They recounted their search for their own identity and their struggle for faith. They recounted their fears and injuries but also their relationship with God and the Church, to which they still felt a connection, despite all the rejection. Their questions and

Queerness IN THE Catholic Church

concerns were genuine and justified, and I felt that a reimagining is necessary! We urgently need to find ways to give these people space within the Church! We must ensure that they are seen and that their questions and concerns are heard.

At the same time, I was studying Pope Francis's encyclical *Amoris Laetitia*. This also made it clear to me: We must no longer exclude people just because they are different or live differently than the Church dictates—or at least, believes it can dictate to them. It is not our task to reshape people according to our ideas but to accompany and include them on their path.

A year later, there was another encounter between that group and me. We wanted to have a biblical discussion, for which I had prepared and printed copies of a text that was to be discussed and brought them with me. To my surprise, however, I discovered that everyone involved had their own Bible with them. It was obvious that these Bibles had not been pulled out of the farthest corner of the bookshelf or newly purchased for this meeting but that they were read regularly. The seriousness with which these people took the biblical message almost shamed me.

I am very happy that we now have our own pastoral Rainbow Ministry in the Dresden-Meissen diocese, which I have officially entrusted to a priest and a parish officer. Once a month, a queer worship service is held in Dresden, which was organized by the people themselves. I have celebrated this service before, as has the Protestant bishop of the region. It is very important to me that the people concerned can decide for themselves which pastoral offerings they want to be part of.

As for the recent ban on blessing homosexual partnerships, I don't want the document in question to be overstated. It is not a papal encyclical but reflects the status quo as formulated in the *Catechism of the Catholic Church*. The statements

Encounter Creates Change

contained in the document are undoubtedly devastating, but they will not be able to remain that way in the long run. There is an urgent need for a reevaluation of queer identities and their life paths in the light of human reason and scientific knowledge.

God's Love Calls Me to Love My Wife

Anonymous
(born in 1970, teacher and social worker)

As a woman, I live with my wife, and I work as a teacher in a Catholic school. This apparent contradiction prevents me from stepping out of anonymity. But I feel that it is time to tell the stories, beliefs, and experiences of violence of Catholics who love the same sex and to make public what the Church expects of us regarding its sexual morality.

I spent almost half my life as a sister in a religious order and worked as a "mother" in a children's home. After twenty-three years, my spiritual journey led me to leave the community. After discovering my new path with God, I was subjected to a humiliating gauntlet from some former sisters. A year later, without giving any reason—but probably because of my homosexuality—and without regard for the children who had been entrusted to me, I was also dismissed from my position in the children's home.

During my time as a religious sister, I had several valuable experiences, for which I am infinitely grateful. I experienced the divine treasure that is the incarnation. But I also experienced unaddressed accidents at work, exploitation of

God's Love Calls Me to Love My Wife

workers, and humiliating psychological violence from superiors and other members of the order. These experiences left me with post-traumatic stress disorder, but I still managed to steer my life in new directions with the power of love.

In the meantime, I am happily working in a school and have found the woman of my dreams. After getting married in a civil ceremony this year and taking part in a Catholic blessing service on May 11, we are now looking forward to the lavish "Festival of Faith and Love" in the Protestant Church.[1]

I once again chose a Catholic employer not because I am naïve but because of my unshakable faith, my desire for a Catholic work environment, and my firm hope for change in the Church's sexual morality: I believe in the love of God that Jesus exemplified for us, which I can experience in the sacraments, but is seen above all in encounters with people and love for them. Every day, I try to bear witness to the fact that every human being is wanted by God, who loves every person exactly as he created them.

God has been able to guide me safely through the many dangerous hairpin turns of my life's journey to find where I can be true to my vocation to love. I still feel God's calling every day, to witness to his work in my life. For a long time, I fought with God about my calling to same-sex love. This path wasn't distant from God, but a path on which I was led by God who accompanied me with his loving closeness.

Based on this powerful experience, I feel that it is time to put away fear and, as I vowed in my religious profession, to say openly with my namesake, St. Mary Magdalene, that I have experienced the love of God, which is stronger than hate, discrimination, and rejection. I experienced it, the love of God, that called me to (same-sex) love. This love is God himself!

---

1. I am unable to locate more information on this *Fest des Glaubens und der Liebe*. Perhaps it is known by another name or is a local celebration without a large online presence.

Committed to the Christian Image of Humanity

Alexander Vogt
(born in 1969, banker)

I was born in Münsterland, both parents Catholic, *CDU*-influenced.[1] My maternal grandfather, however, was Protestant and in the *SPD*.[2] He also had a Jewish mother. My mother was, therefore, more liberal when it came to religion than my father, who came to Westphalia with his parents as a three-year-old refugee from Silesia.[3] The more liberal influence of my mother, who was also a Catholic religion teacher, shaped my two younger sisters and me.

I have always been closely tied to the Church, except for a few years during adolescence. I was (and am) a scout, sat on

---

1. *Christlich Demokratische Union Deutschlands*, the Christian Democratic Union of Germany, a center-right political party. Perhaps the best-known member of "The Union" is Angela Merkel, chancellor of Germany from 2005 to 2021.

2. *Sozialdemokratische Partei Deutschlands*, the Social Democratic Party of Germany, the other major political party in Germany, aligned with the center left.

3. A region in central Europe, today mostly part of Poland. The region was part of Prussia until World War I, when most of it became part of Poland. Silesia was among the first areas invaded by the Nazis during World War II.

Committed to the Christian Image of Humanity

the parish council as a young man, and still participate in our local pilgrimage tradition today, even though twenty-five years ago my job took me to Hamburg and then to Frankfurt am Main. My early faith was also strongly influenced by my elementary school teacher, who was also Catholic.

Today, I work as a banker and honorary federal chairman of the *LSU* (Lesbians and Gays in the Union, that is, in the *CDU/CSU*).[4] And that brings us to our topic. One day, after an interview with my local newspaper, I received a letter from that former teacher that surprised and deeply moved me. She described what happened to her beloved uncle. In the 1950s or 1960s, he lost his job and reputation as a victim of Paragraph 175 of the Criminal Code, which prohibited male homosexuality and was still in effect at the time.[5] It was never discussed in the family.

She congratulated me on my involvement and encouraged me not to let up, because there were still many prejudices in society, in general, but especially in our Church.

My coming out with my parents, the scouts, and thus my old parish was met with mostly positive reactions, and this gave me courage. I know how lucky I was. I am grateful for that. The fact that people in my home parish stood behind me and still stand behind me has undoubtedly helped me to keep my faith in the Church as an institution, along with hope that things will also change for the better in the hierarchy. I am a Christian, and Christians can hope.

---

4. *Lesben und Schwule in der Union*, the Union here refers to the CDU, which is often paired with the other major center-right political party, the *Christlich-Soziale Union in Bayern*, "Christian Social Union in Bavaria."

5. Paragraph or Section 175 of the German Criminal Code was in effect from 1871 to 1994, effectively making homosexuality illegal, categorizing it with bestiality, pedophilia, and prostitution. Hitler expanded it during the worst persecution of gay men in history during the Holocaust, and, despite postwar amendments, it was in effect in both East and West Germany until March 10, 1994.

Queerness IN THE Catholic Church

Today, I look back on more than twenty years in which I actively advocated for equality in the *CDU*, a party committed to the Christian image of humanity as a leitmotif. I've met many who sincerely and seriously try to live out this ideal of accepting humans in their individuality. But I've also met some who cannot even explain what the Christian image of humanity is, despite them so eloquently evoking it. But I still feel most comfortable there politically. And I know that we have achieved a great ideal as the *LSU*.

For this article, I reflected on the number of times I've been confronted with the topic of homosexuality in the context of the Church. There were even more incidents and encounters that I initially remembered. Once again, I had a moment of insight: how great is the ability of an individual — but even more so of a group or organization — to negate, repress, and suppress things!

But at least in Germany, I sense a wind of change. May it not lead to further division but to liberation and acceptance. I often pray for that.

Sanctuary and Snare

Anonymous
(born in 1955, religious priest)

For as long as I can remember, I knew that I was attracted to men. For many years, I did not even know what it was called. It wasn't until my late teens that I came across words like *gay* or *homosexual*. Although I never beat myself up about it, those words hurt for a long time. That's why I tended to avoid them.

I grew up in a rural area and naturally belonged to a clique of boys and girls of the same age; we all knew each other from an early age. I didn't know any other boy, youth, or man who felt the way I did. There was no way I could talk about myself and my feelings. My attempt to tell my parents about it failed because of their nervousness. I tried it only once.

At some point, the first few in my clique began to get girlfriends, but I wasn't interested in that. The only thing I noticed was that the girls liked talking to me, maybe because I didn't want anything else from them. At some point, I tried to have a girlfriend, but it wasn't even a real attempt.

Through my joy as an altar server, I grew into the Church and its worship. I developed great interest and a great deal of perseverance. I took on serving as a substitute sexton and enthusiastically helped in the parish office, even while I was doing vocational training.

Queerness IN THE Catholic Church

In the environment of both the pastor and the young vicar, I found it comforting that I wasn't expected to have a girlfriend. I was relieved of the pressure of having to find a girlfriend. I liked that about the church environment.

It felt good to live in the Church's sphere of influence. I couldn't recognize the dark side of Church at the time. Nevertheless, the prospects for me as a secondary school[1] student were not rosy.

This changed only when I discovered the possibility of studying at a college for young men who might want to become priests. I discovered that there were other men who felt the same way I did, and I immediately fell in love. I was also now learning to talk about myself and my feelings. I didn't beat myself up or wrestle with the Church. It was perfectly clear that a man who wanted to be a priest had to avoid anything sexual. That didn't always work out, which, in turn, led to feelings of guilt.

I chose to live in a monastery. There, I slowly learned to accept my sexuality, to free myself from feelings of guilt, and to be quite grateful that I was gay. There was never a time when I didn't want to be, although living out my sexuality as a religious priest was out of the question for me.

Today I know—both emotionally and theologically—that the way I think and feel is right and shouldn't be anything else. Today, I also know that my existence as a gay man does not call into question my path as a religious priest.

I know that I am connected to and supported in this by many other priests and religious. I am grateful to the Church in this sense: for decades it has given me a sanctuary in which

---

1. *Hauptschule* is an increasingly disappearing form of secondary school in Germany, an alternative to *Realschule* and *Gymnasium*. The *Hauptschule* was originally intended to give a more practical, job skills–oriented education, but enrollment has significantly declined.

Sanctuary and Snare

I have been able to be as I have always been. It freed me from the social pressures of my hometown.

I also feel, however, that the Church and my community, in which I enjoy living as a religious priest, are a kind of snare. I cannot speak openly about myself and my feelings because I want to protect my community. Every now and then I ask myself, "From what actually?"

Queer Life Trusting in God

Dr. Christine Waltner
(born in 1973, teacher)

I didn't choose some things in my life. For example, I was born into a very Catholic family. As a child, it was wonderful but sometimes boring. For example, it was boring when we went to church every Sunday and I didn't understand the homily.

But I liked it when I thanked God for the delicious food in a joint prayer at lunchtime or to have a kiss and the sign of the cross drawn on my forehead by Mama before going to sleep. Praying together made me grateful and invigorated my everyday life.

After getting Sr. Leonara as my teacher in the third and fourth grades of elementary school, I immersed myself so deeply in the Catholic faith that I even wanted to become a nun myself for a short time. I was fascinated and intimidated at the same time by Sr. Leonara and her firm, deep faith. She taught us children a good deal, such as all the parables of Jesus and the stories about him from the New Testament. She understood how to relate these parables and stories to our lives. She made first communion a fascinating highlight for

Queer Life Trusting in God

us. And on Sundays there were worship services in the school church with great guitar music, which was really fun.

But she also gave us a ton of ideas about what to confess. Even as a child, however, it was confusing that I should load so much sin and guilt on myself. And so, I thought desperately about what I could confess. Faith was fulfilling but at the same time a burden.

And that's how it stayed when I found out in my youth that I was more attracted to girls than boys. It took many years to accept my homosexuality, to live it, and to come out—because nobody in the Catholic Church spoke about it. Nobody there, or anywhere else, told us young people that it was okay, that it didn't matter how you felt. I was left completely alone with my feelings.

One of the things that helped me in my time of need was praying to God. And from Sr. Leonara, I knew that Jesus loves everyone and that no one is excluded. I was inwardly at peace with God but not with the Catholic Church. And that's still the way it is today.

I live in a stable partnership with my wife, Almut, and have never felt marginalized because of my homosexuality—except by the Catholic Church. It was even more shocking for me when, in spring 2021, the Vatican Congregation for the Doctrine of the Faith publicly announced that the Catholic Church could not bless homosexual couples because they were living in sin. To me, that is marginalization. In the blessing worship services of #lovewins on May 9, 2021,[1] I felt how it could be, if only the Catholic Church would no longer marginalize homosexuals. It was a very fine feeling, deep inside, that made me imagine what it could be like to be accepted in the Catholic Church, no matter how you feel.

---

1. See "Catholic Means Universal and That Includes Everyone," note 2.

My Faith Gives Me the Strength to Live with HIV

Manfred Weber
(born in 1950, retired)

A lot has happened in my life of more than seventy years. I was born in a village near Ulm, where I still live. I have three wonderful children. My second daughter died in 1980, just sixteen months old, after being in a coma for two weeks. At the same time, my now ex-wife had been in a clinic for four months. My faith gave me the strength to live, the strength to not give up.

That was also the case in 1989, when it was discovered by chance that I was HIV positive. At that time, it was still something of a death sentence. I kept my infection a secret for the first few years. Only my wife, our doctor, and our pastor knew about it. I told our pastor about it because faith has always been very important to me.

Without my faith in Jesus Christ, I probably wouldn't have lived very long. I know he never abandons me like so many people have. I'm still alive today—and sometimes I almost feel like I need to apologize for it. My life doesn't get any easier.

My Faith Gives Me the Strength to Live with HIV

In 2005, I developed cancer, which was undetectable after eight weeks of radiotherapy, but returned in 2013 and could no longer be treated. In 2015, I set out on the Camino de Santiago; I walked 560 miles (900 km) to Santiago de Compostela. Then came the next blow, the cancer had metastasized.

But there are also positive things to report. On the Camino de Santiago, I was preparing for a big step. Although I had doubts as to whether I was worthy, I was allowed to take my oblation in 2016 in the Benedictine Abbey of Königsmünster in Sauerland. That was a very important step for me. In the oblation, I promised to dedicate myself to God, to commit myself to the Abbey of Königsmünster, and to try to live, as much as possible, according to the Rule of St. Benedict outside the monastery.

Since then, Königsmünster Abbey has become something of a second home for me. I can come here again and again and live my faith much more intensively. I feel secure in this faith, that Jesus Christ holds his protective hand over me. He carried his cross up to Golgotha. Why shouldn't I carry my cross too?

I used to have hardly any contacts in the queer scene; I count many good friends there today. How did that happen? After years of hiding, I went public with my HIV infection. For twenty-five years, I was involved in prevention work, gave lectures, took part in worship services for people infected with HIV and AIDS, and therefore got to know all these wonderful people.

Many of them have left the Church. But the way the Church treats them, it's no wonder. I believe in Jesus Christ, but I have my problems with the official Church, because the official Church discriminates against and excludes homosexual people and refuses blessings to homosexual couples. Why should a homosexual partnership be less valuable in the eyes of God than a heterosexual marriage?

I Feel Abandoned by the Church

Anonymous
(born in 1995, chemist)

The Catholic faith has been an important part of my life since birth. I went to a Catholic school and was an altar server for many years. The naturally assumed sense of belonging and always trusting in the Church accompanied me into my young adulthood.

During my college days, I met a woman who quickly became my best friend. I soon realized that I loved her and that she loved me too. Until that time, I hadn't given much thought to my sexuality because I didn't think it mattered who loved who. Our love felt right, and I never suspected the problems it would lead to.

It was easy for me to accept myself for who I am. My coming out was not, however, met with understanding and acceptance from my Catholic family. Their reaction, based on Catholic doctrine, made me feel disgusting and sick. I was told that it is a sin for a woman to love another woman. I couldn't understand what could be wrong with my love. I was accused of having no conscience and developed increasing guilt, insecurities, and doubts about myself and my feelings. In my fear

I Feel Abandoned by the Church

and desperation, I came very close to ending my happy relationship and denying my identity.

At the same time, I felt a growing sense of injustice at being so abandoned by the Church. I became more courageous and gradually came out to my friends. I got only positive reactions and much encouragement from both my believing and nonbelieving friends.

Throughout this whole process, I never doubted God. I have the strong conviction that he loves me for who I am. I just felt abandoned by the Church. Distrust and fear of exclusion grew within me. In a conversation during confession, a priest told me that, to be able to receive the Eucharist again, I would have to leave my partner and recognize my homosexuality as a sin. That hurt me very deeply.

I wish the Church would finally start showing people like me more charity instead of telling them they are inferior and sinful. Being treated like this leaves deep wounds and a lifetime of trauma. Of course, I know that not all members of the Church hold this position, but it is generally tolerated and frequently actively encouraged.

I hope to be part of a parish again where I will be accepted for who I am, where I no longer have to try so hard to hide. That would be a first step in the right direction. Maybe then my trust in the Church could slowly grow again.

The Lord God Wants Me as I Am

Anonymous
(born in 1975, baker)

I remember with horror the day of my first communion: I had to wear a white dress all day! The girls who received their first communion with me were overjoyed in their dresses. But I didn't want to wear one at all and fought against it with all my might—unfortunately in vain.

Even as a child, I was a little punk who didn't play with dolls but preferred to play with cars, was a huge soccer fan, and rode my bike far too wildly. I was repeatedly mistaken for a boy because I cut my hair short and wore boyish clothes. To my chagrin, my parents always "corrected" that and explained that I was a girl.

As I grew up, my grandmothers and aunts gave me all sorts of household and kitchen utensils that they thought I could use on occasions like birthdays and Christmas. As soon as the grandmothers and aunts left, I always angrily flung the stuff in the corner. My parents always gave me presents that I could relate to, for example, toy cars or boys' clothes, just so that every birthday and every Christmas didn't turn into a family nightmare.

The Lord God Wants Me as I Am

There were problems at school too. I especially hated the subjects of home economics and physical education. Why should I learn how to crochet potholders and sew pillows? I hated all that girly crap! In physical education, girls and boys were separated, so, of course, I had to go with the girls. I could hardly get into rhythmic gymnastics and dance. Instead, I would have preferred to run riot in volleyball and track and field.

I found my puberty very uncomfortable; I stood in front of the mirror and saw my breasts grow. But it wasn't me. Then, when my period started, I thought I would have to come to terms with being a woman. I tried to suppress everything else because I believed I shouldn't be the way I felt. My mother used to say, "The Lord God wanted us to have a girl."

Then my mother developed a brain tumor and died. Everything got worse for me because I now had to do more housework than ever before—cooking, cleaning, washing. At some point, I felt like I was suffocating with it all. I started therapy and tried a few things. I found that I hit it off more with lesbian women than with men. What I wanted was a family—a family where I was the husband and father.

In 2010, I became aware of a book called *Blue Eyes Stay Blue—My Life*.[1] It was written by Balian Buschbaum, whose deadname was Yvonne; he was a successful pole vaulter before he came out as a transgender man. After reading this book, I knew, "I am a man too."

The late abbot of the Benedictine Abbey of St. Boniface in Munich, Odilo Lechner, helped me a lot. One time, he told me, "The Lord God speaks to you like the voice on a GPS. If you are on the wrong path, it says with the same friendly voice, 'Please turn around!' That's why you can go your way full of peace. The Lord God is always with you!" And that's exactly what I did.

---

1. Balian Buschbaum, *Blaue Augen Bleiben Blau: Mein Leben* (Frankfurt am Main: Krüger, 2010).

www.ingramcontent.com/pod-product-compliance
Lightning Source LLC
Chambersburg PA
CBHW071419160426
43195CB00013B/1747